triathle

Guide to
SPRINT
& OLYMPIC
TRIATHLON
RACING

Chris Foster

with Ryan Bolton

VELO.
press

Boulder, Colorado

4745 Walnut Street, Unit A
Boulder, CO 80301-2587 USA

VeloPress is the leading publisher of books on endurance sports and is a division of Pocket Outdoor Media. Focused on cycling, triathlon, running, swimming, and nutrition/diet, VeloPress books help athletes achieve their goals of going faster and farther. Preview books and contact us at velopress.com.

Distributed in the United States and Canada by Ingram Publisher Services

Library of Congress Cataloging-in-Publication Data

Names: Foster, Chris, 1982- author. | Bolton, Ryan, author.
Title: The triathlete guide to sprint and olympic triathlon racing / Chris
    Foster with Ryan Bolton.
Description: Boulder, Colorado: VeloPress, 2020. |
Identifiers: LCCN 2019053444 (print) | LCCN 2019053445 (ebook) |
    ISBN 9781948007078 (paperback) | ISBN 9781948006200 (ebook)
Subjects: LCSH: Triathlon—Training.
Classification: LCC GV1060.73.F67 2020 (print) | LCC GV1060.73 (ebook) |
    DDC 796.42/57—dc23
LC record available at https://lccn.loc.gov/2019053444
LC ebook record available at https://lccn.loc.gov/2019053445

This paper meets the requirements of ANSI/NISO Z39.48-1992 (Permanence of Paper).

Art direction: Vicki Hopewell
Photographs: Front cover, Jesper Gronnemark; back cover, Warren Little/Getty Images
Cover design: Dave Allen
Illustrations: Oliver Baker

20 21 22 / 10 9 8 7 6 5 4 3 2 1

CONTENTS

INTRODUCTION

I am a triathlete. That is to say, I *became* a triathlete. I wasn't born one. I didn't grow up with goggles, a helmet, and a pair of running shoes gifted to me in a transition bag on my fifth birthday. As a kid, I played outside. I rode BMX bikes. I ran around and played flashlight tag.

When it came time for the elementary school mile test, I "practiced" really hard in my Airwalk skate shoes, running around my house until I got too tired to keep going. All in the day before the run itself. Despite my best efforts to sabotage the result, I did really well—after all, at my school the faster you finished the mile, the quicker you got to lunch. All said, the concept of being first to get food probably drove much of my athletic career. I was an accomplished cross-country and track runner in high school; then I later willed my way onto the running program at Penn State, where an old-school coach took a chance on someone who probably should have never made the team as a freshman. But by the time I was a senior, I was one of the top guys on the squad.

In the summers during college, my athletic restlessness (and boredom) sparked my interest in a sport that combined two things I really liked (running and cycling) with one thing I really didn't (swimming). Though I had swam back in high school, our team was more like a swimming club (I usually trained in board shorts), and I never liked it. No one would ever call me a "swimmer" without using air quotes.

I set my sights on the Dewey Beach Sprint Triathlon—an approximately 800-meter swim, 15-mile bike, and 3-mile run. Despite a decided lack of skill and enthusiasm, I went out to the Atlantic Ocean near our house in Delaware to try to swim for as long as I could to prepare for it. At first, I could only go a few minutes at a time. With no walls to hang onto or rest intervals between sets, the choppy, salty water basically had its way with me. Finally, I was able to swim 1,000 meters without stopping. But it was hard, and I didn't like it.

I got my hands on a Schwinn 10-speed that was way too big for me and fitted it with some crazy horns that triathletes called "aerobars." I don't remember much about the bike except that those aerobars were a super cheap pair from Profile. They were so cool to me then, I still remember the make and model.

When the day came, I wore my old maroon high school Speedo from start to finish. I suffered mightily through the ocean swim; my thighs chafed raw during the windy bike on the flat, sandy expanse of Delaware's Route 1, and on the run, I passed dozens of people, but I was too tired to care. I don't remember much about the finish except that Queen's "Bicycle Race" was playing as I went to collect my bike.

But I finished the damn thing. And then I slept the rest of the day like I had just gotten back from Mount Everest. I had never been so tired in my life. My result wasn't amazing—it didn't foreshadow a professional career, or even show promise of someone who could win their age group. It just made me really, really tired. But I liked that.

HOOKED

Triathlon was a puzzle to me. I was a good runner, but I didn't run very well during the race. I was a decent cyclist, but guys older than my dad rode by me like I was out for a walk. As for swimming, I'm pretty sure the lifeguards had marked me as a drowning risk. But I was hooked by this gnawing sense that I *should* be faster, that I *could* be faster, if only I trained more and if I trained better.

I longed to crack the code of how to go *faster* and how to finish and not be comatose for the following 10 hours. I certainly improved upon the former, even if I've never mastered the latter throughout my 10 years as a professional triathlete and an editor at *Triathlete*.

So why is my story important to you—the aspiring triathlete-to-be, the mid-level multisporter aiming to improve, or the seasoned iron-vet looking to continue the sport without depleting finances, schedule, relationships, or career? Because I wasn't born a triathlete, and neither were you, we *become* triathletes by training for swimming, biking, and running. Then we race. Then, we decide how to take the next step: Do we want to go longer until we hit our body's "distance ceiling"? Do we want to go faster until we've tapped our potential at a given distance in all three sports at once? Do we want to make friends, live a healthier lifestyle, renew a sense of athletic pride that maybe we haven't experienced for years or maybe ever? I found all of these things in the years since that first sprint tri, and if you're reading this book, there's a good chance you might too.

KNOWLEDGE IS POWER

I went into my first race not knowing much aside from the distances I had to complete and the order of events. I had no training plan, just an idea that I should do the distance of each leg a few times each week if I wanted to survive.

Had I known a little more about training, I certainly would have performed better, and probably had a lot more fun. It took me years to understand that having a plan was more important in triathlon than any other sport I've done before or since. But I needed more than just a plan. With swimming, biking, and running all acting as moving targets bouncing off each other, getting the formula right is a little bit like playing with a chemistry set—you get the mixture wrong, and *boom* you're in trouble.

That challenge and balancing act are also what makes triathlon so fun. Great swimmers get humbled on the run, great runners get humbled in the water, and great cyclists sometimes get humbled in both. You push a little too far in one, another gets out of whack. You don't do enough in any of the three, and you suffer on race day. You overdo it in all of them and you run the risk of burning out completely—the human body can only handle so much. Still, it's possible that we can learn to get better—excel even—at three very different sports. This is why triathlon is worth doing and worth doing with your best foot forward.

Solving this multisport Rubik's Cube is what bonds triathletes together. Yes, we're racing against each other when the gun goes off, but there's really only a handful of triathletes in the world at any given moment who have their body's magic formula figured out. Ask anyone in the transition area how their training has been going, and there's always something: "My run has been going great, but I've got this shoulder thing . . . " Or, "I've been putting in tons of swimming, but I haven't had as much time to bike as I'd like." (Time is the great enemy of triathletes, and we'll get to that later.) Figuring out how to balance swimming, biking, running, strength training, nutrition, hydration, rest, recovery, overall health, motivation, family, and work life is a monumental task, but it's also the thing that binds this weird tribe together.

Finding a healthy balance among those 12 things is one of the main reasons I opted to go *faster* rather than *longer*. I believe in the healthy, well-rounded version of the multisport lifestyle that exists in short-course racing.

Training and racing in relatively shorter bursts, and eschewing six-hour rides for shorter, more intense workouts, not only keeps energy levels up and a body's structural integrity in check, but it also allows the athlete to have a life outside of the sport—with the time and energy to enjoy it.

Triathlon can open many doors—whether it be to personal satisfaction, overcoming fears, meeting new people, changing a lifestyle, becoming healthier, or conquering new challenges. But triathlon can also become physically and mentally isolating if approached the wrong way. Just like the chemical reaction described earlier, triathlon can have dangerous outcomes, or it can create something beautiful. If you want to learn how short-course triathlon can positively transform all aspects of your life, this book will be your guide.

You'll be joined on your journey by experts with a deep, wide knowledge of short-course racing and how to excel at it.

Ryan Bolton, one of the experts featured in this book, coaches the entire range of triathletes and runners, from Olympians to age-groupers to first-timers. The former pro triathlete and Olympian has degrees in exercise physiology and human nutrition, and in 2018, he was named USA Triathlon's high-performance technical adviser.

Though he coaches both short- and long-course athletes, his true passion lies in short-course racing because he believes the shorter time commitment and increased intensity are a healthier fit for today's athletes.

Ryan is responsible for much of the technique work in the book and also designed the training plans, which are rooted in a coaching philosophy that prioritizes three key ideas: periodization, polarization, and race-day specificity. *Periodization* is progressive, systematic cycling of a training program with different phases at different times in the season. *Polarization* is the focused combination of very easy efforts and very hard efforts. And *race-day specificity* is the idea that we should train as we intend to race. Underlying it all is Ryan's foundational belief in the well-rounded athlete, where a balance between life and training is struck in a way that sets up success in both.

You'll also benefit from the wisdom of **Casey Maguire**, a physical therapist, former triathlete, and current cyclist. His career is devoted to getting people—athletes and nonathletes—back to doing the things they enjoy. Some of his favorite patients are triathletes because they're rarely lacking in motivation (although unfortunately they're often lacking in restraint!).

Casey urges all athletes to make a consistent commitment to a flexibility program—which you'll find in these pages. He believes passionately in a training program that creates a strong base of core stability, general flexibility, and strength to allow speedwork to flourish. His emphasis on not overdoing volume and always respecting recovery makes him the ideal PT contributor for a short-course racer's guide.

HOW TO CHOOSE A PLAN

Back in the days of trying to figure out my place in the multisport world, I knew pretty quickly that I enjoyed shorter, more intense training sessions over longer, slower-paced workouts. The beauty of triathlon is its versatility, meaning we can do lots of types of races at lots of different distances—you don't have to choose just one. But to truly excel at a distance—and get the enjoyment that comes from doing something well—you need to understand and focus on its unique facets, not merely the mileage in the training plan.

To the new triathlete reading these pages: Short-course racing is a perfect introduction to this multifaceted, challenging sport. Shorter distances allow for quicker, safer adaptation, more fun, more free time, and more experimentation with training and racing. You may hear about someone whose first tri was a long-course race, but no coach worth his or her salt would recommend that pathway to someone who isn't already extremely proficient in all three sports. The information and Level 1 Program in this book will get you safely and healthily to the short-course start line—hopefully with a newfound love for the sport and the triathlon community.

Or maybe you've already done a handful of multisport events and now find yourself thinking about how you can improve your performance. The best way to get better at triathlon, regardless of which distance you settle on, is to work on all the other ingredients *before* adding more volume. Just like in chemistry, getting the formula right is important before concocting something bigger: A little "pop" may no big deal, but a big explosion certainly is. This book's Level 2 Program offers a good balance for you, increasing the workload and the challenge enough to see gains, but not so much that you find yourself injured before you even get to the start line.

Finally, if you're a veteran triathlete who craves pure speed in short-course and are seeking to find your limit without just going longer and longer, the Level 3 Program is for you. This advanced plan is designed for those who want to go faster than they ever have before. Bear in mind, you don't have to be a top age-grouper or pro to use the Level 3 Program, but you do have to want to get the absolute best out of your short-course racing—and be willing to do the work to get there.

The information and plans contained in this book will help any level of triathlete, whether you've been in the sport for years or are entirely new to it. Our objective is not necessarily to build world champion pros, but rather to help push you, wherever you are in the sport, to a new personal level of growth.

We want you to get faster than *you* already were. This might also make you faster than everyone else you used to compete with; however, that's more of a fun side effect than the goal. Whether you're brand-new to multisport, dropping down in distance to try your hand at short-course racing, looking to race short to get better at long course, or simply looking to make triathlon a more well-rounded and healthy part of your life, the plans in this book offer you the tools you need to reach your goals.

BECOMING THREE-DIMENSIONAL

The expert knowledge in this book is useful for athletes across the ability and experience spectrums, from new to seasoned. Though you may want to use the book as a reference, dipping in and out of sections to find the information you need the most, we recommend reading the chapters in order, as information early on serves as a foundation for the building blocks that come later. Beware of shortcuts. Unequivocally, the best way to excel at triathlon is to take the time to learn about the ancillary stuff: refining technique, devising a race-day strategy, warming up and cooling down effectively, and committing to a solid, consistent strength training routine, alongside the nitty-gritty execution of the mileage in the training plan itself. We strongly believe in the concept of a "whole triathlete" when approaching training and racing—another reason to love short course: It gives you time to work on these details!

Although I was a collegiate runner, I really never learned anything about proper running form until years into my pro triathlon career. As a post-collegiate runner, I remember training for my first marathon, thinking that as long as I followed the training plan, I'd crush the race. I spent no time learning about the difference between racing a 10K (the longest I had raced up until that point) and a marathon, the different strength training needed to remain injury-free, or the differences in form, pacing, recovery, and nutrition that a marathon required. I showed up on the starting line that day in "good shape"—or in what I thought was good shape, based on the miles I had run.

When the gun sounded, I took off, right at the front with the leaders. I ran through the city blocks waving to the crowd who had gathered outside, sure I was going to make some prize money. A race had never felt so easy to me—until it didn't.

What I failed to understand as I cruised through the half-marathon mark at the pace required to hit the Olympic Marathon Trials time, was that I needed to take in both nutrition and water, and that I wasn't physically prepared for the latter stages of the race. At mile 16, my legs started to hurt. By mile 18,

I was having a hard time keeping my running form together—something I had never even considered up to that point. I had to stop and walk a few times, which had never happened in my entire running career. As the miles went by and the race left me behind, I was reduced to a walking, stumbling mess. The undertrained stabilizer muscles in my legs and core caused imbalances to develop in real time, and I was walking so hunched over and with my feet so splayed outward, my now-wife nearly cried when she saw me waddle through the finish chute. It took two IVs and weeks of recovery to bring me back to normal. What had happened?

I was a veteran who had made an all-too-common rookie mistake. I thought that because I was hitting all of the miles and times in my training plan, I didn't need anything else. My arrogance at being a good runner blinded me to the reality of what I was undertaking, and I had failed to lay down a proper foundation—essentially the third dimension—to my one- or two-dimensional training plan.

Years later, I now know a lot more about form, strength training, and technique, and guess what? I have become a faster and better runner in my 30s than when I was training full-time at 21. My cycling also saw improvements from adding these dimensions: I was cycling faster, yet easier, and I was running off the bike better thanks to that form work. But it was my swimming that saw the most striking difference.

In triathlon, where time is at a premium, you need to be working smarter first, harder second. This means not only doing everything you can to train, but also doing every part of training just right. You wouldn't practice a piano piece as fast or as hard as you could without paying attention to the notes you were playing, right? Triathlon is the same way.

We want to help you fill in those gaps you might have had in your training, or maybe areas you never knew you needed help with. You'll work smarter by not just following the plans but also learning about the ancillaries required to put your best foot (or arm or pedal) forward.

Here's a quick overview of how this book is organized:

1. **THE BACK STORY.** Triathlon is relatively new, and the original pioneers of multisport were far from the kitted-out pros you see today. We'll take a quick trip through triathlon's origin story, as well as look at all the reasons why short-course racing is a smart choice.

2. **THE GEAR.** Triathletes love stuff. And while you can easily amass a houseful of gear if you choose, here we will break down the essentials that will help make you fast as well as ease your journey on race day.

3. **THE TECHNIQUE.** Form and technique are vital to becoming a good triathlete, and entire books are dedicated to learning the form that is required to do just one sport. We'll focus on the keys to winning technique and common tri-specific problems that can lead to injury or underperformance.

4. **THE SUPPLEMENTARY WORK.** A successful triathlete needs to do more than just swim, bike, and run in order to improve and stay injury-free. Here we offer advice and tips on strength training and injury prevention, which will help strengthen the glue that holds your basic training together.

5. **THE STRATEGY.** Different triathletes at different stages of their racing career need to approach race day with very different plans. Here we will lay out some simple strategies that will help keep surprises at bay and prepare your mental game.

6. **LEVEL 1 16-WEEK PROGRAM.** This training recipe will take you from day one to the finish line. The plan is broken out into a calendar with each day's workouts organized into four key "phases." Each phase has an introduction to arm you with an understanding of why you're doing what. We'll also talk about next steps after your race—how to transition from "completing" to "competing."

7. **LEVEL 2 16-WEEK PROGRAM.** This plan is for those who have done a few races and want to improve their times. You'll find more advanced concepts, such as different ways of measuring effort that are more precise than in the Level 1 Program. We'll also discuss what it means to be shooting for performance rather just finishing. This program has more volume, more intensity, and different workouts than in Level 1. While we keep time manageable in Level 2, this plan will require more commitment than in Level 1 without getting to the pointy end of Level 3.

8. **LEVEL 3 16-WEEK PROGRAM.** This is a roadmap to lead you to finish *at your very best*. The plan is also intended for those looking to get the most performance out of their body at a shorter distance, in order to become a more well-rounded person and make triathlon a more manageable time and energy commitment. You'll learn how to go fast, not just far. We'll look at how to "change gears" from simply *doing* triathlon to focusing on fast and discuss what will look different if you are dropping down in distance. We'll explore the new sensations that short-course-specific training will bring and how to approach a proper short-course taper. Finally, we'll discuss race-day strategy and how to get ready for your fastest short day ever.

9. **APPENDIXES.** Here you'll find more detail on test sets for swimming, biking, and running; swimming drills; running drills; and strength training.

Now we know where we're headed. It's time to start putting the pieces together. Let's go!

YOUR
SHORT-COURSE
TOOLKIT

1

THE BACK STORY

Let's start with a few definitions.

A triathlon is a swim, a bike, and a run, usually completed in that order. Unlike other 'athlons, such as modern pentathlon, heptathlon, and decathlon, triathlon competitors race from swim to bike to run without scheduled breaks between events. The term "multisport" also applies, which includes duathlon (biking and running only) and aquathlon (running and swimming only), among others.

While the order of a triathlon is pretty standard, the distances vary widely. The most popular race formats, with fastest finish times, include those in Table 1.1. Those finish times are inspiring but, of course, most of us can expect to spend at least 50 percent more time racing than the pros, depending on skill level.

Rules sometimes vary by distance or event; however, a few simple ones always apply: Triathletes are required to provide their own equipment, complete the racecourse, and finish without accepting support from outside sources. We will take a deeper dive into the rules later (see p. 90), but

TABLE 1.1. The Tri Dosage

EVENT	DISTANCE	PRO PODIUM
Short-course		
Super sprint	Anything below sprint distance	– – –
Sprint	750-meter swim, 20K bike, 5K run; often half-Olympic distance	Under 1 hour
Olympic	1,500-meter swim, 40K bike, 10K run	2 hours
Long-course		
70.3	1.2-mile swim, 56-mile bike, 13.1-mile run	3.5–4 hours
140.6	2.4-mile swim, 112-mile bike, 26.2-mile run	8 hours
Ultradistance	Anything beyond 140.6 distance, including double or triple iron-distances	– – –

rest assured that nowhere does it say that triathletes have to be fast, own specialized equipment, or possess a deep knowledge of the sport. That said, there is certainly room to geek out on history, equipment, or speed, and learn everything there is to know about the nuances of this complex and beautiful sport.

A (VERY) BRIEF HISTORY

Though not essential to competing in your first or fastest tri, knowing a little bit about the history of the sport helps athletes of any level understand that triathlon is simultaneously distinguished and weird, old and new, and definitely ever-changing.

Neither as ancient as wrestling nor as new as e-sports, triathlon is considered a temperamental teenager in the annals of sporting history. Taken separately, swimming, biking, and running each has roots in different places in time. The first competitive running events may have begun as far back as 1800 B.C.—though it's possible people were racing even before then. Swimming came along much later, with the first recorded swimming competitions credited to the British in the early 19th century. Cycling is the new kid on the block, with the first documented cycling races occurring in mid-19th century France.

Putting all three together in its current recognizable format is often credited to a ragtag bunch of San Diegans in Mission Bay on September 25, 1974. A natural extension to the biathlons (running then swimming, at the time) that the San Diego Track Club had been hosting as an alternative to track workouts in the early 1970s, Jack Johnstone and Don Shanahan created and directed the first version of triathlon that traces its bloodline to current-day tri.

That first race was a novel mixture of swimming and running—totaling 500 yards and 6 miles respectively—with a continuous 5-mile bike ride in the middle. Participants were told to "bring their own bike," and many of the 46 competitors used beach cruisers. Most showed up with little or no tri-specific training. The event proves that triathlon's start was far from slick or fancy. The first steps toward slickness would come four years later, when two race participants, Judy and John Collins, created the Hawaii Ironman®, a sport that would take triathlon from those scrappy margins of Southern California out to the entire world.

So yes, the first recognizable modern triathlon was a sprint! And while its current version is an entirely American sport, there is evidence of early triathlon in Europe as well. The French had been racing what they called *les trois sports* ("the three sports"), *la course des débrouillards* ("the race of the experts"), and *la course des touche à tout* ("the race that touches everything") since at least the beginning of the 20th century. Though it appeared in various distances and orders of swim, bike, and run, it's nonetheless widely recognized that these events were still confined to our modern version of "sprint distance."

GOOD COMPANY

Short-course triathlon made its biggest splash on the world stage with its inclusion into the Sydney Olympic Games in 2000. And thanks to its continued run of success and growth worldwide, in 2020 the Tokyo Olympics will expand the triathlon program with yet another short-course event—the mixed relay. The mixed relay format will include two females and two males per team, with each participant completing a 300-meter swim, a 7.4K bike, and a 2K run before handing off to the next teammate.

Though many people think of long-course racing—particularly the iron distance—when they think of triathlon, short-course racing is arguably more competitive on the professional level. In fact, of the 18 men who finished in the top three at the Ironman World Championships between 2008 and 2018, 10 of them were serious short-course athletes prior. Of the 15 women who finished in the top 10 during the same period, seven were serious short-course athletes prior. Across the tri world, athletes of all abilities can count themselves in good company when they line up on the starting line of any short-course triathlon.

WHY GO SHORT?

Super sprint, sprint, Olympic, 70.3, 140.6, ultra—with so many distances in this multifaceted sport, it's easy to get lost in the different "tribes" within triathlon. Short-course racing is sometimes viewed as an event for first-timers or for pros looking to race at the Olympics. Some make the mistake of thinking that iron-distance racing *is* triathlon and you're not a triathlete until you finish 140.6 miles in a day.

But the reality is that if you are a triathlete who races Olympic and sprint distances, you are actually a part of the largest group of triathletes in multisport. According to a 2016 survey from USA Triathlon (USAT), fully 61 percent of its members do Olympic-distance racing or shorter.

> I love that you can race short-course more frequently than long-course racing since the recovery time is so much shorter. If something goes wrong in a short-course race, like a mechanical, poor pacing, or a nutritional miscalculation, you can jump back into racing as soon as the following weekend.
>
> —Two-Time Olympian Sarah True

Today, short-course racing is seeing something of a renaissance. Over the past decade, Olympic-distance and shorter races have grown in popularity, with rising participation not only of everyday triathletes, but also of those looking to test their competitive chops. The inclusion of women's short-course triathlon as a provisional NCAA sport in 2014 showed that national governing bodies like USAT and even institutions of higher learning are willing to inject not only their school's name into the sport but also resources.

In 2014, the NCAA held its first official NCAA Women's Triathlon Championships, and while the sport has seen a strong collegiate club scene for decades, the legitimacy of the NCAA has brought even more weight to short-course racing in the US. Each year, there are national collegiate events—for both NCAA-level triathletes and for those on the club level. This flourishing ensures that the next generation of triathletes will almost certainly grow up in short-course racing—and hopefully stick around for a long time.

Accessibility

Another key reason for short-course's growing popularity is its accessibility to and for a broad range of athletes. The barrier to entry for short-course is much lower than in long-course. First, consider the entry fee. You may be able to borrow a bike and scrounge up running shoes and basic swim gear, but there's no way around paying to start a race. The 70.3-distance races generally start at $300 and go up from there; iron-distance races run in the

$600 and up range. Fees for short-course races, on the other hand, rarely climb above $200.

Furthermore, the race fee doesn't reflect many of the additional costs of triathlon: equipment, nutrition, training, and more, which all become more critical (and expensive) the longer the distance. Equipment is more specialized as the distances increase; nutrition is needed in higher quality; and then there are the travel costs, with long-course racers often requiring a longer stay away from home to accommodate for their acclimatization and the longer race days.

With shorter race and training distances along with lower entry fees, short-course events are a better choice for a wider swath of athletes. Want to see the most diverse group of triathletes? Look no further than a short-course race.

A Matter of Time

Short-course racing is also more accessible to those with limited time resources. In an increasingly busy world where time can be even more precious than money, many athletes are looking for the most bang-for-their-workout-time buck. While an iron-distance training plan requires an average minimum of 16 to 18 hours per week—and that's just to *complete* a race, not to race it—the beginner sprint plan in this book requires a *maximum* of 13 hours per week or less to get from couch to start line. As for veterans, when you factor in the fact that elite-level long-course athletes will train on average 20 hours per week to compete at a high level, the 15 hours per week in this book's advanced-level plan is like a drop in the bucket.

And if racing is important to you, you'll find that short-course racing offers you leeway for more events. Even the most optimistic long-course coaches don't recommend racing more than about three times per year. The demands of training for those events—building a base, building strength, tapering, then maintaining that all over again—alongside the physical toll of the race itself make doing multiple long-course races in a season a risky proposition.

With short-course racing, however, not only can you race more, but you can employ different strategies and techniques on race day with less chance for season-ending repercussions. If something doesn't work out and you blow up, you can plan another race soon. In fact, that may be the greatest bonus of short-course racing: the luxury of really going for it and seeing what happens without the penalty of having to wait another month or two to try again.

Balancing Act

No matter how you slice it, triathlon is a demanding sport. Whatever the distance of your race, the sport will take up far more time than simply competing in running, swimming, or biking events. Pursuing triathlon will require attention to keeping the important things in your life—such as work, family, and friends—in balance.

That balancing act is particularly grueling in long-course. As Coach Bolton puts it to his long-course athletes before they begin training: "Once you start training for long-course triathlon, there will be three things in your life: triathlon, family, and work. One of those three things will have to suffer."

When you're training three to eight hours per day, there is little room for anything else and very little of a buffer for your health. Overtrain a little bit too much in an already long training schedule and the repercussions can take weeks to fix. The line is razor thin when you're racing for 70 miles-plus, and the truth of it is that "fit" doesn't always mean "healthy."

In 2018 I went to Hawaii to cover the Ironman World Championships for *Triathlete*. If you've never witnessed the event firsthand, it's a sight to see. Thousands of athletes, the best long-course triathletes in the world, converge on Kona and, in a matter of days, the population of this otherwise sleepy town grows by nearly 50 percent, its new inhabitants all tri-crazy.

A day or two before the race, I was in a taxi, making casual conversation with the driver. He asked if I was in town for the race, and I told him I was covering it for the magazine. He nodded, replying, "It's interesting how the town really changes on race week—I've never seen so many healthy people in my life!"

I looked out the taxi window at the people walking down the sidewalk, and it dawned on me for the first time in roughly 15 years in the sport: There wasn't much *healthy* about the way some of these people looked. Sure, they looked "fit," and eager to race. But some were not so much striding as hobbling, with what was clearly some sort of injury. Others looked tired, gaunt, and stiff. Many looked weather-beaten, and a few looked like they could use a hot meal. I was looking at literally the fastest long-course athletes in the world, yet it didn't appear to be a particularly healthy crowd. Perhaps it's because there is a cost for being very, very good at one very narrow thing. The specificity required to be so good at long-course triathlon unfortunately comes at the cost of being a well-rounded person. Whereas triathlon is supposed to make you a complete athlete, the extremely long hours of training required to get to Kona undeniably leave gaping holes in an athletic repertoire.

Part of the appeal of short-course is that it's easier to strike a balance between life and sport. You are able to dedicate less time to swimming, biking, and running, and more time to ancillaries such as strength training, technique, and the specifics that make you a multifaceted multisporter. This makes you not only less prone to injury, but leaves the door open to all sorts of other sports and pursuits. The things we do for short-course tri actually make us better at so much more!

Give Me a Break

One of triathlon's biggest selling points is that it offers a mental and physical break from pursuing a single sport. But nevertheless, as in any sport, injury does occur, and while there are a bevy of factors that can predispose you to injury, the most common refrain from experts in avoiding injury is to play an active role in your own injury prevention. Doing certain routine exercises is key. We'll share some of those movements in this book, but here's the thing:

They only work if you take the time to practice them *before* it's necessary to seek professional help.

And there's that time thing again. Doing these strength exercises takes time, time that you'll have when you adhere to a balanced short-course plan; time you might not have if triathlon has already pushed itself to the edges of your schedule's allotment. Ironically, those who race long need strength training and prehab/rehab the most, yet they're the ones who have the least amount of time or energy to get it done.

Fitness for Real

Recalling my taxi ride through Kona and the scene on the sidewalk, the people I saw were certainly "in shape" for an iron-distance event, but were they truly "fit" by any real-world standard? We're learning more and more about the way the human body responds to exercise, and some of those findings are challenging conventional theories on physiology. Gone are the days of "more is more," as sports scientists discover that shorter, more intense intervals are actually more beneficial to increasing cardiac output.

Nowhere is that more evident than in the world of high-intensity interval training (or HIIT). Paces need to be mixed up, increased at some times—with adequate rest—and decreased at others to prepare for more intense training that will "lift" an athlete's potential output and prevent the dreaded plateau.

We'll get into the hows and whys of interval training over static, steady-state training, but the prevailing wisdom today falls more in line with the training and the racing that occurs in short-course triathlon. Though the racing is faster—and potentially tougher at times—today's science says that the physiological gains are greater through this higher-intensity style of sport than we ever knew before.

This thinking not only applies to triathletes looking to improve their times and places, but it's also important for those who are looking to improve their health and lifestyle. For example, weight loss can come at a more consistent, sustainable rate when training and racing doesn't require every last ounce of our energy. A more balanced lifestyle is easier to achieve when the scales aren't so close to tipping into the overtraining zone.

The Need for Speed

Let's not forget about two more important aspects of short-course triathlon: It's fast, and it's fun! For those who like the feeling of the redline, short-course tri puts you at swimming, biking, and running speeds that are far faster than that of its longer, slower cousin. The thrill of an aggressive swim pack, the excitement of passing throngs of cyclists as you whiz by, and running fast and with the kind of freedom and joy you might have left behind in elementary school are intangibles that can be deeply motivating, far beyond ticking off mileage and checking off boxes. Tom Cruise's character in *Top Gun* doesn't "feel the need for an eight-hour bike ride," now does he?

TRADE LONG FOR STRONG

The benefits of short-course apply whether you're new to the sport or have been in the sport for years. In fact, for all the reasons listed, many veterans are finding their way back to short course after years of pursuing longer distances.

Maybe short-course racing is going to be your new home after years of going long, or maybe short-course is simply a great detour to rekindle your love for competition or get a jump-start off of a training and racing plateau. As more and more triathletes find long-course racing to be too time-consuming, too expensive, too lonely, and too delicate to balance, there's a lot to be said for dropping down in distance.

It's our goal to show every triathlete—from beginner to intermediate to advanced—how to push their training to the next level, a faster level, at a shorter distance and with greater health benefits.

Remember, you're never *just* doing a sprint- or Olympic-distance event. With its rich pedigree, broad accessibility, and opportunity to be fiercely competitive should you choose, short-course racing—in all of its forms—has a lot to offer.

Instead of thinking of short-course triathlon as strictly a stepping-stone to a longer distance, this book will show you that "racing short" can be whatever you want it to be: a place to begin, a place to stay and remain well-rounded and healthy, and a place to go when you're looking to take your triathlon training and racing to the next level.

Let's get started!

2

THE GEAR

Triathletes have three sports to juggle, and so not surprisingly, there can be a lot of gear. Note we said "can be" not "has to be." Because when it comes to gear in triathlon, you have a choice. You can keep it simple, going with the absolute essentials and eschewing the rest, or if you're someone who loves to geek out on cool toys and tech, then there's definitely a place in triathlon for you, as well.

In most cases, triathlon-specific gear isn't just cool (though it often is). Rather, it can make you faster, more comfortable, and even let you have more fun. Once upon a time, triathletes had to make do by shoehorning swim-, bike-, and run-specific equipment into this brand-new multisport. Today, however, there is a whole industry dedicated to tri, with choices that are practically unlimited.

Short-course triathlon, in particular, has some of the widest options when it comes to gear designed to make you fast, comfortable, and more in control. Equipment made for long-course tri works just fine for shorter races, although the inverse is rarely the case. In fact, "making do" with non-tri gear is far more feasible in short-course than in long-course. Since the distances

> I love that mistakes are that much more costly on the short course. It means you have to be that much more focused and "on" to win.
>
> —2016 Olympian Ben Kanute

and time spent racing are shorter, we need fewer specialized things. Want to do your first tri with just cheap goggles, a mountain bike, a helmet, and a pair of running shoes? Do it. Want to do a long-course race like that? Ouch.

Products and technologies are constantly changing, but in the pages that follow, we've broken things down into the essentials that every athlete needs along with pieces of gear that will help take your training and racing to the next level. Alongside each piece, we've rated its ability to impact you in four key categories: comfort, safety, speed, and injury prevention. The ratings go from 1 (no impact) to 5 (high impact). Use this to help you navigate all of the choices according to your priorities and spend money on what's important to you. If you are new to triathlon, you can skip over the advanced gear and avoid buying things you don't really need. We've also noted where some gear is great for training but not allowed in racing.

SWIM

Goggles

COMFORT **5** // SAFETY **4** // SPEED **4** // INJURY PREVENTION **3**

Every triathlete should invest in a good pair of goggles. If you can't see on race day, it doesn't matter how much training you've been doing, as you'll be spending most of the swim trying to clear your goggles and spot the swim buoys. We strongly recommend goggles with a large field of vision, as opposed to minimal pool goggles, as you need to be able to spot not only what's in front of you, but also objects in your periphery, such as other people and obstacles. Start with clear lenses, but because of changing conditions outside, it's smart to invest in a dark-tinted pair for bright sun and a colored pair that highlight things like buoys in overcast conditions. They should fit tight enough not to leak, but not so tight that you get a headache. Antifog coating is a must.

Swim Cap

COMFORT **5** // SAFETY **2** // SPEED **3** // INJURY PREVENTION **1**

A swim cap is a must for both men and women. Not only will it keep hair from tangling and getting "fried" by the chlorine in your training pool, but there's also a pretty significant performance effect of keeping that tangle of hair in place in the water. Another bonus? If you train in chilly water, a cap—particularly a neoprene one—will keep your head warmer and core temperature higher, which allows you to spend less energy trying to keep your body warm. Since we are all about training with race-day specificity, it's important to get comfortable with putting the cap on and swimming in it during every workout. A cap is also usually a race-day necessity that's often included in your packet with your race number. Race directors require them to see who's who, what swim wave you're in, and for safety.

Wetsuit

COMFORT **4** // SAFETY **2** // SPEED **4** // INJURY PREVENTION **1**

If the water is warm enough (as a rule of thumb, water above 75 degrees Fahrenheit will be comfortable without a wetsuit), you can race without a wetsuit. However, comfort aside, a swim wetsuit (not a *surf* wetsuit—yes, there's a difference) will not only keep you warmer, which means less energy expended staying warm, it will also give you a fairly substantial performance benefit. A wetsuit helps to float your body, placing you in a more hydrodynamic position. Some wetsuits, especially less expensive ones, may cause some restriction through the shoulders, so be sure to try it on first. And don't forget that you'll have to take off your wetsuit post-swim and that the clock will be running. Practice as much as possible with your wetsuit, both swimming and disrobing, to ensure that the time you save in the water isn't lost in transition. You can't afford it, particularly in sprint tri!

Tri Suit

COMFORT **4** // SAFETY **1** // SPEED **4** // INJURY PREVENTION **3**

The best thing about a tri suit is that you can wear it from the start all the way to the finish line. While not a race requirement, a tri suit is quick-drying and hydrodynamic enough to swim in, padded enough to bike in, and has a pad that's light enough to run in. In short-course racing, where every second counts, wasting time putting on or taking off clothing is a luxury. Available in one- or two-piece styles, look for a tri suit that has a comfortable pad you wouldn't mind running in, a few pockets if you want to carry nutrition on the bike or run, and a zipper that's easily accessed so you can open the suit up when you get hot.

Body Lubricant

COMFORT **5** // SAFETY **2** // SPEED **2** // INJURY PREVENTION **3**

There are two types of triathletes: One who hasn't tried body lube yet, and one who uses it all the time. "I never use body lube, I tried it, and I don't like it," is not something you will ever hear from a triathlete. Trust us. It's inexpensive, and it helps with all of those little spots that rub and chafe while swimming (neck, armpits, lats), biking (underparts, feet), and running (underparts, feet, armpits, lats, pecs). Train with it, so you can learn which hotspots require body lube. Insider tip: Putting body lube around the wrists, ankles, and feet of your wetsuit will help you remove the wetsuit in transition, but be sure to practice. Also be sure to use a body lube (*please* don't use cooking spray) that won't damage your neoprene investment.

Sunscreen

COMFORT **3** // SAFETY **5** // SPEED **1** // INJURY PREVENTION **5**

A good, broad-spectrum sunscreen is important for anyone who trains or races outside, and as a triathlete, you'll be outside a lot. Look for something that's both water- and sweat-proof, as you'll be covered in one or the other near-constantly. Also be sure it's something you enjoy putting on. Spending a little more money on a sunscreen that smells nice and doesn't make your skin look or feel chalky will make you more likely to put it on before every training session. Spray sunscreen works well for an uncovered back that's hard to reach.

ADVANCED SWIM

Training Paddles, Pull-Buoy, Band

COMFORT **2** // SAFETY **2** // SPEED **3** // INJURY PREVENTION **4**

When used together, these three training items are a great way to focus on form while working on pulling strength. When used separately, they provide different specificity: Paddles help with shoulder strength—begin with smaller sizes and work up over time to prevent strain; a pull-buoy helps float the legs and quiet kicking, simulating a wetsuit, and also helps with pulling strength; a band (or old bike tube tied in a loop) prevents kicking, forcing you to work on body position in an extreme way while simultaneously working on strength. Note: for training only.

Kickboard, Fins

COMFORT **1** // SAFETY **1** // SPEED **3** // INJURY PREVENTION **4**

These two training items work similar areas. When used together, a kickboard and fins are an excellent way to cool down and warm up, and work on your kick, body position (when combined with a snorkel), and ankle flexibility. When used alone, the kickboard helps build that excellent swimmer's kick described in the swim technique chapter (see p. 46), generating power from the hip, not the knee, and avoiding scissoring. It also helps you work on body position with your face in the water. Fins can be used alone to work on improving your swim tempo and your ankle flexibility and reducing strain on the shoulders while swimming during recovery or when rehabbing injury. Note: for training only.

Snorkel

COMFORT **3** // SAFETY **2** // SPEED **2** // INJURY PREVENTION **3**

A snorkel is an essential tool for working on proper swim technique. In short-course training, which has less volume than a long-course program, you need to be sure that you are using every minute to get better. A snorkel helps you focus on head and body position by removing the root of most swimmers' problems: breathing. Without the need to turn the head for a breath every few seconds, a swimmer can focus instead on holding the correct body position in the water, where the head is, arm/elbow position, and specifics of the catch phase. Note: for training only.

Speedsuit

COMFORT **3** // SAFETY **1** // SPEED **4** // INJURY PREVENTION **1**

While a wetsuit will make the vast majority of swimmers faster by helping with floatation and body position, there are times when a wetsuit isn't the best choice. In short-course, sometimes the swim is so short that the amount of time to take off a wetsuit is not worth the gains in the water (this can often be remedied by excellent transition practice, which we'll discuss later, see p. 102), and sometimes a wetsuit isn't legal (or prudent) because of the water temperature. In these cases, a speedsuit—or a swim skin—can be worn over your tri-suit on race day and will provide a more hydrodynamic surface, better muscle compression, and/or reduce drag. A speedsuit is meant to be worn almost solely on race day, should be worn over your racing tri suit, and can be quickly taken off in T1.

BIKE

Bike

COMFORT **4** // SAFETY **3** // SPEED **4** // INJURY PREVENTION **3**

Every triathlete needs a bike. But bear in mind, the rule isn't "Participants *must* have a super-fast bike." You can race a short-course triathlon on basically any bike that has brakes. At a local sprint race, you'll see everything from $15,000 race bikes to beach cruisers and BMX bikes. Obviously you'll be much faster on a tri-specific bike—meaning something with aerobars, a forward-position seat angle, thinner road tires, deep-dish wheels, and a carbon frame—but it's not required. We'll spell out details on a more specialized bike in the advanced section below, but the ideal basic setup is a road bike—with thinner tires and at least 20 speeds—that's been sized or fitted at a bike shop. (Bought it used? Ask a local shop if they can fit or size you for a fee.) Have a pro look it over to ensure it's tuned up and in safe order. Aerobars are a good upgrade for comfort and speed, but a comfortable saddle should be the first upgrade on your list.

Helmet

COMFORT **3** // SAFETY **5** // SPEED **3** // INJURY PREVENTION **5**

A CPSC-certified helmet (look for a sticker on the inside of the helmet) is a requirement to race any USA Triathlon event, and yes, they do actually check for this. Be sure your helmet has that sticker, otherwise it can be a problem on race day. With the exception of some newer concussion-prevention technology like MIPS, a more expensive helmet will only be more lightweight and/or more ventilated—not necessarily safer. Even the less expensive helmets today—think under $100—are still very good. Teardrop-shaped aero helmets and round, smooth-looking aero-road helmets discussed in the advanced section are strictly for speed and rarely very comfortable or ventilated.

Bike Shorts

COMFORT **4** // SAFETY **2** // SPEED **1** // INJURY PREVENTION **3**

Padded and tight-fitting, even an inexpensive pair of bike shorts is light-years ahead of regular running or athletic shorts—trust us. Look for something that is tight enough not to sag, but not so tight that your legs feel like over-packed sausages—this might cut off circulation. The pad should be substantial enough to provide comfort on your saddle, but not so big that it causes chafing. These shorts are best used for everyday training and left at home in exchange for a more-minimally padded tri suit on race morning.

Flat Kit

COMFORT **2** // SAFETY **4** // SPEED **2** // INJURY PREVENTION **2**

A flat kit is important to anyone who will be riding outside where flat tires are inevitable. However, the one thing more important than a flat kit is knowing how to use one! Check out online videos or ask an experienced cyclist for help. Knowing how to work on your specific bike is a huge asset when you're stranded on the side of the road. In addition, get either a portable pump or a CO_2 inflator, and a replacement tube—alongside other standard flat-changing gear, like tire levers. Don't waste time with a patch kit as they can be unreliable and user-error is pretty common, unless as an absolute last resort.

Water Bottle

COMFORT **2** // SAFETY **2** // SPEED **4** // INJURY PREVENTION **3**

Remaining properly hydrated is essential to triathlon racing and training. You should be adequately hydrated before you even begin a workout, and you'll need to keep up your water and electrolytes intake throughout the workout. The same applies to racing, and if you bring your hydration along with you on the bike or run, you'll save time by not stopping at aid stations. Keep in mind, we train with race-day specificity, so anything you do during race day, you'll want to practice plenty of while you train.

Sunglasses

COMFORT **4** // SAFETY **3** // SPEED **2** // INJURY PREVENTION **3**

The best sunglasses will give you a wide field of vision, not fog up, and—just maybe—give you a dose of tri style. There are a plethora of options that will work, from dirt cheap to wildly expensive, but even cheap pairs should at the very least be shatterproof with UV protection. While runners tend to have a variety of preferences when it comes to sunglasses, cyclists almost universally like sunglasses not only for keeping the sun off their eyes but also for wind and debris protection while riding.

ADVANCED BIKE

Aerobars

COMFORT **4** // SAFETY **3** // SPEED **5** // INJURY PREVENTION **3**

Though this could arguably be a tri basic, a set of aerobars is absolutely essential to the more advanced multisporter. Not only will the tighter elbow position present less surface area to the wind and get you in a lower upper-body position overall, but when properly fit, it can also help you produce more power comfortably. Carbon bars will not only be lighter than aluminum, but also better at smoothing out bumps in the road. The most important thing when choosing an aerobar is finding one with lots of adjustability unless you're confident in your exact aero position.

Power Meter

COMFORT **1** // SAFETY **1** // SPEED **4** // INJURY PREVENTION **2**

For advanced racers, a power meter is essential. We'll get into the different methods for training measurement and benchmarks in the program sections of the book (see pp. 111–115), but in sum, power on the bike is one of the most important ways to objectively measure output for training and for maintaining pacing while racing. Consider a single-sided power meter if you are looking to save money while still getting the training and racing benefits of objective output; look for a dual-sided power meter if you want to enjoy the extra tools that help explore pedaling efficiency with deeper analysis of your form. Where you implement your power meter on the bike is up for debate based on different needs, but look for a power meter that you can use consistently while both training and racing for the best results.

Bike Trainer

COMFORT **1** // SAFETY **4** // SPEED **1** // INJURY PREVENTION **3**

A bike trainer may be the most important piece of cycling equipment that an advanced short-course athlete can buy for efficient training. Though often very boring and tiring, time spent on the trainer is optimized because it is raw training without distractions like coasting downhill, lights, or traffic safety issues. Users simply clip in, get in the aero bars (which is also an excellent way to practice your aero position), and grind away. While good for even long rides, using a bike trainer is particularly effective for fast training with specific intervals that short-course tri demands.

Tri-Specific Hydration System

COMFORT **4** // SAFETY **3** // SPEED **3** // INJURY PREVENTION **2**

There are many different styles of systems that can go almost anywhere on the bike: between aero bars, on the downtube, behind the saddle, and a few others. But the most important characteristic of any tri-specific hydration system is that it allows you to drink without moving drastically from your position. When set up properly, this allows the rider to drink more (greater capacity) and more often (easy access), all while staying in an aero position out of the wind. Different bikes require different solutions, though the most popular systems are placed between or on the aero bars.

Tri-Specific Bike

COMFORT **4** // SAFETY **3** // SPEED **5** // INJURY PREVENTION **3**

A tri-specific bike is crucial for any triathlete looking to take his or her short-course racing to the next level. While tri bikes are certainly more aerodynamic—with carbon (ideally) or aluminum tubing that creates a shape that slices through the wind more effectively—there's more than meets the eye. An actual tri bike (not just a time trial bike) is set up with a unique geometry that puts the rider in a more forward position over the pedals. This helps engage a different, more powerful group of muscles, allowing the rider to "save" other muscles for the run. Tri-specific bikes also allow for a greater variety of aerodynamic positions and sometimes have built-in hydration systems (see previous entry). A good carbon frame will also reduce road vibrations (as well as reduce weight), which allows riders to train longer with less fatigue and run off the bike with more energy. The most important thing when buying a tri bike? Fit. Triathletes should *always* get fit by a professional: A $10,000 bike without a fit is far worse than a $2,000 bike with a good, pro fit.

Deep-Rimmed Carbon Wheels

COMFORT **3** // SAFETY **1** // SPEED **4** // INJURY PREVENTION **1**

For simplicity's sake, in this category, we're talking about carbon-rimmed wheels with a depth of 30mm to 60mm—the rim depth that still gives you an aero benefit but also works well on hilly or windy courses. But as a general rule of thumb, the deeper the wheel, the faster it will go in a straight line (assuming no unpredictable side winds), but the heavier it will be, and usually the more rigid, comfort-wise. Also, deeper wheels are more sensitive to crosswinds, and lighter riders should practice often with their deep wheels to become comfortable. Look for clincher or tubeless-ready tires, and avoid tubular rims that need to be glued.

Disc Wheels

COMFORT **1** // SAFETY **1** // SPEED **4** // INJURY PREVENTION **1**

Disc wheels—whether full carbon or wheels with a wheel cover—have fallen slightly out of fashion. They can be heavy, uncomfortable, and frankly, expensive for a race-day-only piece of gear. But for the purposes of the advanced short-course athlete racing on a flat to moderately hilly course, a rear disc wheel can be an excellent choice because of its extreme aero advantage at higher speeds. Also, with advances in disc brakes and tubeless tires, many of a disc's downsides have been eliminated. Bear in mind that because a disc wheel is solid, it can be difficult in a crosswind for lighter riders, but the depth of the carbon wheel up front actually has more of an effect on handling. Also, because of a disc wheel's heavy weight, riders will need to push harder on hills, but the disc's weight holds momentum better, so riders will need to adapt their style to "push through" the bottom of hills, ideally "flattening them." Be sure to train with your disc from time to time to perfect this technique. Triathletes who average above 20 miles per hour will find the greatest benefit from a disc.

Aero Helmet

COMFORT **2** // SAFETY **1** // SPEED **4** // INJURY PREVENTION **1**

An aero helmet is a race-day-only piece of equipment that is all about squeezing seconds off of your bike split. Of course, it's important to train with your aero helmet from time to time (a good head position with a given aero helmet is worth more than its weight in gold), but an aero helmet makes the rider faster by reducing the thing that creates the most drag on the bike—you. In choosing an aero helmet, think about the reality of wearing it—can you maintain the necessary position—and the logistics of where you race, as aero helmets often have minimal venting for better aerodynamics, and can be quite hot. Aero helmets can sometimes increase comfort because they cover the ears to reduce sound, keep your head warm in chillier conditions, and sometimes have built-in visors that negate the need for sunglasses.

RUN

Race Belt

COMFORT **2** // SAFETY **2** // SPEED **4** // INJURY PREVENTION **1**

In most multisport events, race directors require that you wear a paper number (most likely along with a timing chip) on the run and possibly also the bike leg. Rather than wasting time pinning the number in transition (and you certainly don't want it flapping around in the swim or bike if not required), you can use a race belt, which is an elastic belt with your number already attached that can be quickly clipped around your waist. Because it is so inexpensive and the alternative would take up so much time in a short-course event, this little thing should be considered an essential.

Running Shoes

COMFORT **4** // SAFETY **2** // SPEED **3** // INJURY PREVENTION **4**

The proper shoe for your personal running style is crucial to preventing injury and training effectively. Because of the amount of training you'll be doing in your shoes, be sure to invest in a pair that you know work for your body. Go to a reputable running-specific store if possible, rather than to a general sporting goods store or online shop. Ask the salesperson for help choosing a shoe based on your gait, your intended use, and your comfort level. Most importantly, be sure to run for at least two weeks on new running shoes before race day. Even if you see a shiny pair at the race expo, save them for the next tri!

Heart Rate Monitor

COMFORT **1** // SAFETY **2** // SPEED **3** // INJURY PREVENTION **2**

A wireless heart rate monitor is essential for objective training-effort measurement. For the purposes of this book's Level 2 and 3 Programs, readers should look into getting a heart rate monitor that is chest-strap based, as wrist-based heart rate monitors are not as accurate, particularly for the more intense interval workouts that require consistent and reactive measurement. (Note: In the Level 2 and 3 Programs, we'll help set up heart rate zones that'll serve as the benchmark for the entire plan.)

ADVANCED RUN

Racing Flats

COMFORT **2** // SAFETY **1** // SPEED **4** // INJURY PREVENTION **2**

The term "racing flats" is meant to encompass any pair of lightweight training or racing shoes that a triathlete would use on race day or for fast training, such as tempo runs or intervals. Racing flats' biggest benefit is their lighter weight—usually at the expense of cushioning and/or support—but racing flats can also give you a mental boost: When a triathlete puts on racing flats, he or she knows it's time to get serious. Some racing flats also have special technology designed to help propel the runner forward, and many racing flats will actually feel faster because of the reduced cushioning that allows for a faster cadence and more proprioception.

Speed Laces

COMFORT **3** // SAFETY **2** // SPEED **4** // INJURY PREVENTION **2**

Speed laces are inexpensive accessories designed to replace shoelaces in your race-day shoes. Speed laces let the shoes sit open in transition, allowing you to slide your feet in quickly in T2, and then pull them tight and secure them in one motion before setting off onto the run. Though this should be practiced many times before race day, the proper use of speed laces can not only shave off seconds in transition, but also help a triathlete distribute more even pressure on the top of the foot when putting on shoes in a hurry.

Running Power Meter

COMFORT **1** // SAFETY **1** // SPEED **3** // INJURY PREVENTION **3**

A running power meter is usually a small pod attached to the wearer's shoe or something already embedded into a smartwatch. Unlike cycling power meters that measure force applied to the pedals, cranks, or hub with gauges, most running power meters use complex formulas to calculate running "power" based on foot contact time, stride length, cadence, and a host of other factors, depending on the brand. For those who run on trails or extremely hilly terrain, these devices do a great job of giving an objective level of output regardless of conditions—something minutes-per-mile pace can't always do. This is also excellent for pacing on race day, particularly if the course is hilly or has lots of twists and turns.

OTHER EQUIPMENT

Foam Roller

COMFORT **3** // SAFETY **3** // SPEED **1** // INJURY PREVENTION **4**

A foam roller is a simple physical therapy tool that helps prepare muscles for a workout or race and can be an invaluable aid when it comes to injury prevention. A roller can and should be used frequently and after workouts in other sports as well. The basic idea is that athletes use their own body weight to apply pressure to troublesome spots, slowly moving themselves over the roller in an effort to "dissolve" knots and tight areas. For short-course athletes, if you buy only one piece of recovery/injury prevention equipment, this is the one.

3

THE TECHNIQUE

Proper technique is crucial to becoming a proficient (and fast!) tri-athlete. But with three very different sports to contend with, refining those winning techniques is a challenge. When you're a single-sport athlete, you only have to focus on technique and form for one sport, but when you're a triathlete, you need to balance three different types of technique that are, at times, at odds with each other; the best way to swim has little to do with the best way to bike; the best way to run has little to do with the best way to swim.

Form becomes even more important in short-course racing than in long-course because you are going much faster and as such won't be able to rely on just "grinding it out" over long distances. Every stroke, every turn of the pedal, and every step you take should be as close to perfect as possible to maximize both your training and your speed. The good news is that with short-course racing, where workouts are more difficult than they are long, you have extra time to focus on swimming, biking, and running correctly.

Entire books have been written on swimming, biking, and running technique, so here we'll spend our time focused on the biggest and most damaging flaws and challenges that typically affect triathletes. We've selected key areas in each sport that, if worked on, will reap huge dividends in your training and short-course racing.

SWIMMING: SWIM RIGHT, THEN SWIM FAST

Swim coaches see a handful of common swim technique mistakes time and time again. While triathletes who don't have a swim background will want to read this section closely and carefully, even former competitive swimmers should review these points, as the observations, tips, and tricks collected here are open-water specific—meaning this is how you need to swim in the unique conditions of a triathlon that exist without lane lines, walls, or personal space. In short-course, the swim is exceptionally dynamic. With more bodies nearby, less space to spread out, and less time to fix mistakes, it's crucial to work on your open-water skills, becoming a great open-water swimmer first and a pool swimmer second. This advice also bears in mind that unlike in pure competitive swimming, short-course triathletes will need to bike immediately after getting out of the water, with less time afforded to "settling in" to the bike.

Technique Flaws and Fixes

Head Too High, Body Too Low

Humans aren't designed to live in the water. Our very human nature tells us, instinctively, when we first plunge into the wet stuff that we need to breathe at all costs and keep our heads above water. While this is great for surviving, it is not so great for swimming. When you tilt your head too far out of the water, your hips go down, just like a seesaw. This is highly inefficient and unnecessarily saps strength, a bit like swimming while dragging a giant anchor. Yes, you need to lift your head to sight, but it's important to consciously readjust your body position after each sighting, with the aim of keeping yourself streamlined and long.

The fix ▸ Spend quality time swimming with a swim-specific snorkel. This device allows you to play with your head position in the water without fear of—to put it simply—drowning. Practice looking at the bottom of the pool and forcing your hips to ride higher in the water. Even without a snorkel, practice breathing on each side (yes, both sides for open water, discussed in more detail later in this chapter) while letting only half of your face come out of the water. This takes a little courage, but it's essential to maintaining proper swim position.

Elbow Drops at Entry

In swimming, the "catch phase" occurs during the first third of the underwater pull and initiates your power. It is arguably the most important part of the stroke, as an efficient catch allows you to pull as much water as possible. The technique becomes even more important in open-water swimming because you often need a high elbow to get above waves or other swimmers. Coaches commonly see swimmers dropping their elbows— particularly when fatigue sets in—failing to successfully "grab" the water during this phase, which compromises their power. It's essential to get this technique right.

The fix ▸ A good catch starts before your hand even touches the water. Concentrate on keeping your elbow high, and imagine reaching over a barrel as your hand enters the water—this isn't just good form, it's crucial for many rough-water swims. Then visualize moving your body over and past your hand, rather than sliding your hand past your body. The difference is subtle but important. When done correctly, you will activate the correct strong muscles in the back. The one-arm swimming drill is a good way to train this concept. See p. 242 for instructions on the One-Arm Drill.

⚠ Poor Catch

A poor catch sets up poor technique from the beginning of the underwater phase and reduces propulsion at a critical point of the stroke.

The fix ▸ **One-Arm Drill** (p. 242), **Side-to-Side Drill** (p. 242)

⚠ Crossing Over

Crossing over happens when your hands or arms cross the centerline of your body at hand entry. It inhibits proper alignment from hands to shoulders and prevents a proper catch.

The fix ▸ **Tarzan Drill** (p. 244), or simply swimming with paddles

⚠ Weak Kicking, Kicking from Knees, Flexed Feet, Poor Ankle Flexibility

While you may have heard that kicking isn't important for triathletes (that wetsuits cause enough lift to negate kicking or that less kicking saves energy for the bike and run), don't believe it. A good kick will help you swim faster and more efficiently in three ways: It creates lift to help with the body position issues discussed above; it helps with body rotation, providing stability and balance; and it helps propel you through the water. But *how* you kick matters.

Many triathletes, particularly runners and cyclists, tend to flex their feet, rather than point their toes, which renders the kick ineffective and also creates a huge amount of resistance in the water. This is most often a result of bad habits or poor flexibility. Another common issue is scissoring, when your legs remain stiff like scissors when kicking, and weak kicking, when you fail to use your legs enough for propulsion.

The fix ▸ Fixing your kick is crucial to smoothing out the swim stroke, and it will make you more efficient and ultimately faster. To get a stronger kick, spend time kicking with a kickboard and focus on building better kick strength. To stop scissor kicking or to eliminate a kick generated from the knees rather than the hips, kick with an alignment board—a small pointed kickboard—and a snorkel. Also use a snorkel to work on alignment simultaneously by eliminating the need to turn your head and breathe. **Vertical kicking**—kicking in an upright position, hands at your sides and keeping your head above water— also helps with alignment. Be sure to use a freestyle kick (not breaststroke or eggbeater). Finally, sitting on your feet, with the tops touching the ground, for a few minutes a day can help with poor ankle flexibility.

Not Varying Speed and Stroke Rate

Working on high-end speed can sometimes fade from a swim program simply because it's difficult—which is precisely why it's important. In open-water swimming, different conditions require different stroke rates— for instance a strong current or waves will require a shorter, choppier stroke. Furthermore, some swimmers have been (incorrectly) taught to swim with as low a stroke rate as possible.

The fix ▸ Our programs mix in high-end speed sets with low yardage and high recovery. This is bread-and-butter sprint triathlon training stuff. You can work on a dragging stroke rate by counting your strokes and shooting for 55 to 70 strokes per minute. Work both ends of the spectrum to ensure you're comfortable and ready for any conditions that come your way.

Cadence Issues

A cadence that's too low can require too much strength, and one that's too high can cause an excessively high heart rate or poor form. In open water, you will want to increase stroke rate to better move through chaotic waters. Stronger, more powerful swimmers can be on the lower end of the cadence range.

The fix ▸ Practice the following stroke count set:

Swim 50 meters/yards near threshold pace counting strokes.

To calculate your stroke rate: Stroke count / time (in seconds)

For example, if you swam the distance in 45 seconds and took 40 strokes, that's 0.89 strokes per second, or 53 strokes per minute (40/45 = 0.89, 0.89 × 60 = 53).

Swim 5 × 50 at the same pace (with 30 seconds rest), but play with your stroke rate to achieve the optimal range of 55 or higher.

⚠ Underestimating Technique, Form, and Drill Work

Bad habits are a result of lazy or poor technique. Even if you've been a triathlete for years—or perhaps *because* you've been a triathlete for years—your form is probably not perfect. The longer you go without addressing technique issues, the harder it can be to fix them. While most of us would much rather be running, swimming, or cycling and consider drills about as fun as going to the dentist, remind yourself that drills are your secret weapon—the thing that will set you apart from all those other triathletes who mistakenly skip them.

The fix ▸ Make drills a part of every workout you do. Whatever level of swimmer you are, beginner or Olympian, compile a list of your unique "technique limiters" and build a drill program around those. See Appendix B, p. 241, for drill ideas and instructions.

⚠ Breathing Rhythm Is Off

When you breathe at the wrong time of the stroke phase or exhale too little underwater, your breathing rhythm is off. If you don't fully exhale underwater, you'll need to exhale when it's time to breathe above water. This can cause undue lift and time spent above water, causing you to drop the hips and impacting the proper rhythm of your stroke.

The fix ▸ Spend time at the start of each swim set working on **Bilateral Breathing** (see p. 51). You can also try the **Bob Drill**. Bob up and down in the pool, focusing on exhaling completely as you go down, inhaling when you're up. After a few rounds, swim normally but focus on exhaling completely while your face is in the water.

⚠ Neglecting Open-Water Training

Training with "race specificity" means training like you race. Very few triathlons take place in a pool with flip turns and your own private lane. So just as you wouldn't show up to a race riding a bike you've never ridden before, why would you expect to be able to successfully swim in open water without having specifically practiced for it?

The fix ▸ Doing every single workout in open water may be neither practical nor possible for many people. For those athletes who don't have access to open water, it is crucial to spend at least one—ideally two—sessions per week in the pool simulating open-water skills. How? Work on sighting a specific object on the pool deck a few times per length during a set, get in a lane and swim alongside some fellow triathletes, or swim at a pool without lane lines and practice swimming in a square with lateral turns. Open-water skills practice is so important that we've devoted a whole section to it.

The Water Is Open

As triathletes, we are nearly always training to race in the open water. This means that all of your swim training, even if done in a pool, should be done with open water in the back of your mind. Remember, the element of open water will affect not just where you race but *how* you race.

Here are six areas to focus on that commonly give triathletes trouble when transitioning to open-water swimming from pool swimming, along with tips and tricks to help ensure they don't trip you up once the gun goes off. Understand these and master the fixes, and you will be well on your way to not only a faster swim split, but far greater comfort and confidence in the water, no matter what race day brings.

Stroke Rate

In the pool, your stroke rate can mostly remain a constant for a given distance; however, in the open water, rough conditions call for different approaches. Traditionally, swimmers who excel in 50-meter pools have longer, lower stroke rates than those who do well in 25-meter pools. You might think that means a lower stroke rate is better in the open water where there are no walls or flip turns, but the opposite is true—particularly in sprint events.

The fix ▸ Though it can feel uncomfortable at first, practice stroke rates up to 75 strokes per minute in the pool to become more versatile in the open water and more ready for rough conditions. Rougher water or a bigger, more aggressive pack requires a higher stroke rate; calm water and swimming solo means you can lengthen out your stroke and conserve energy.

Sighting

In open water, there are no lanes or black lines to guide you, so triathletes need to become experts at sighting. On race day you'll be expected to pick out a small buoy or landmark, possibly hundreds of yards away, so practice this skill and work it into the rhythm of your stroke. If you swim in a zigzag on race day, no matter how fast you are, you'll be losing precious time.

The fix ▸ The best way to refine this skill is to swim in the open water and find small landmarks to sight during your swim. If a pool is all you've got, look for a water bottle or object on the pool deck. In order to make sighting a fluid, less speed-inhibiting part of your stroke, lift your head vertically as low as possible—the water line should be just above your nose—and once you've spotted a "snapshot" of the object, turn your head to the side you feel most comfortable breathing on. Do not lift your face or even your mouth completely out of the water, as this action will drop your hips. As for frequency, you will need to alter how often you sight depending on conditions, so work on sets where you sight sometimes every other stroke and sometimes every seven strokes.

⚠ Bilateral Breathing

While some coaches may encourage breathing to only one side—a few very famous swimmers have developed a "hitch" that takes advantage of this one-sided technique—we believe that for open-water swimming and for swimmers who do not have the benefit of hundreds of thousands of yards of swimming to develop a special technique, bilateral swimming (breathing on both sides while swimming) is your best option.

The fix ▸ Bilateral breathing is a crucial technique for triathletes to practice and master. This method will balance out your stroke—removing any right or left side preferences—and allows for increased awareness of other swimmers, obstacles, and buoys in the open water. This balance helps you swim in a straighter line, preventing you from wandering all over the swim course. Also, in ever-changing open-water swim conditions, sometimes it becomes essential to breathe on one side for some of the swim and then later on the other side, for example when the sun is rising or with an aggressive swimmer on your side. Not having to wait for the preferred breathing side to lift up your head to sight makes you more versatile and nimble as conditions change. While working on breathing drills on your "off side" is a great way to start, the best way to become comfortable with breathing on both sides is to do it with intention and build it into your stroke. Start with bilateral breathing during your warm-up and cooldown; then add it into pulling sets before finally integrating it into your main fast sets.

Wetsuit Practice

Wetsuits are legal in most races with water temperatures below 78 degrees. While a wetsuit provides warmth—key both for comfort and energy conservation—it also provides a unique advantage for most swimmers. The increased buoyancy provided by a swim wetsuit's neoprene (note: do *not* use a surf wetsuit unless you have no other option) also corrects body position by floating the body higher in the water, particularly the legs and hips. Downsides are the restriction some swimmers might feel in the shoulders, especially with lower-end wetsuits, and the discomfort some might experience if they tend to overheat, but unless you fall into those categories, swim times with a wetsuit are almost always faster than without.

The fix ▸ If most of your races are wetsuit legal, then neoprene is an essential piece of equipment. If possible, find a local shop that carries a few options to try on because the fit will vary from brand to brand. Most importantly, be sure to practice with the wetsuit as much as possible prior to race day. Don't feel strange wearing it for pool workouts, and be sure to rehearse taking it on and off quickly.

Going with the Flow

Currents and conditions in the open water are always going to be a factor, and understanding how they work can be the difference between a bad swim and a great one. In addition, it's important to understand the water's entry and exit well before race day. Race day surprises are not something you need.

The fix ▸ Do some information-gathering about the body of water you'll be competing in: Will the water likely be rough or calm? Warm or cold? What time of day will it be when your wave goes off; where will the sun be? Look to lifeguards and locals to help you familiarize yourself with current direction (which can affect sighting and swimming in a straight line) and the ground underwater or waves around where you'll be entering or exiting the water. This information can go a long way toward easing some stress and wasted energy on race day.

Drafting

In cycling, you may hear the term "drafting" used as a four-letter word, but in triathlon swimming it is an essential skill. Also called "getting on feet," swim drafting is the easiest way to get faster without extra physical effort at all.

The fix ▸ Drafting involves swimming as close as possible to the person in front of you (without constantly tapping their toes) and is perfectly legal in the swim. Ideally, in a race, after a few minutes of swimming, you'll settle into an appropriate group of swimmers with a similar speed. Use this opportunity to locate someone who appears to be swimming straight, and follow their bubbles. A good way to practice this is to enlist the help of some friends to take turns leading and following in the pool or open water during a few sets. This is a skill that takes time to get comfortable with, so be sure to set aside some pool or open-water sessions to get it done.

CYCLING: MORE THAN MEETS THE EYE

Proper form and technique on the bike are essential for any triathlete, regardless of distance. But when you're racing Olympic-distance and below, it's even more important to be efficient and confident on the bike because shorter courses are often compact with tight twists and turns and little time to make up for mistakes.

Many triathletes are surprised to learn that there's much more to cycling than mashing down on the pedals. In this section, we'll look at five key areas: pedaling, cadence, bike fit, bike position, and handling.

Pedaling

Just as the best swimmers look effortless in the water, the best cyclists look like they're floating when they ride. Aim for a smooth pedal stroke and a quiet upper body. This will ensure that you're using your finite energy supply only to pedal the bike, not to wrestle it into submission. While this elegant form may take years of riding to develop, it starts with analysis and then deliberate work to refine the technique.

Powerful pedaling requires that you be clipped into the bike. If you don't have clip-in pedals, you won't be able to pull up properly, sacrificing your power, which you cannot afford to do. It takes some practice to feel comfortable clipping in and out of pedals, so make sure you start riding with them well before your event.

The pedaling cycle itself can be broken down into four phases. Review these phases carefully and begin to build awareness of when you are in a particular phase during your stroke cycle so that you can focus on executing it properly.

PHASE 1 (12 O'CLOCK TO 4 O'CLOCK): This is the most powerful phase of the pedal stroke because you can use your weight to aid the major muscles like the quads and glutes to produce force. In this phase, focus on dropping your heel, not pointing your toes; the foot should be 20 degrees from flat at the top of the phase, gradually flattening by 3 o'clock. This process, known as "ankling," doesn't come naturally and requires deliberate work to develop.

PHASE 2 (4 O'CLOCK TO 6 O'CLOCK): By 4 o'clock, your ankle should start angling back up to that 20-degree mark, arriving there by the time you hit 6 o'clock. You're still using the quads and glutes, even as the calves and hamstrings start to take over. At the end of this phase, you will begin transitioning from pushing down on the pedals to pulling up.

PHASE 3 (6 O'CLOCK TO 10 O'CLOCK): The most difficult phase in the pedal stroke, here you'll engage the calves and hamstrings even more. Though it will feel like you're pulling up through the pedals, it is actually centrifugal force that is pulling your foot up and over. The best thing to do is think about "getting out of the way" to let centrifugal force do its thing, so imagine releasing the muscle rather than engaging the opposite one. Your ankle should still be 20 degrees from flat.

PHASE 4 (10 O'CLOCK TO 12 O'CLOCK): At 10 o'clock, think about pedaling over the top of the circle, pushing through to the end of the phase at 12 o'clock. You should have your downstroke ready to go, so try to initiate that action early in this phase and prepare to transition from a 20-degree ankle angle to the slight heel drop in phase 1. This final phase can be particularly challenging for those with hip mobility or other weakness.

You can observe these phases by placing a mirror next to your indoor trainer. Not only should you be thinking about your legs and ankles moving around a circle, it's also important to visualize your legs pushing down and pulling up in a straight line. If your knees are bowing out or inward as you look down at your pedal stroke, you're not only wasting precious energy that should be going straight down to the pedals, but it could also indicate an imbalance or oncoming injury.

Cadence

Once you've refined your pedal stroke, you'll want to fine-tune *how often* you're pedaling with that great technique. Just as in swimming, you should apply a different cadence to different situations: On a cold day, you might choose a higher cadence to keep your core temperature up; many cyclists prefer a higher cadence while pushing into the wind as well. On the flip side, you may want to use a lower cadence on long descents or when you have a tailwind. Experimenting with cadences in training will help you be nimble under the varying circumstances that race day can present.

There is an ideal cadence range for efficiency in triathlon. Aim to pedal with a cadence between 85 and 95 rpm. The easiest way to determine your own cadence without a cycling computer is to count how many times your knee comes up in 15 seconds and then multiply by four. Less than 85, and you'll be sapping your leg strength, wearing them out needlessly for the run; more than 95, and your heart rate will likely be too high and you're burning too much energy. That high cadence requires more cardiovascular output, requiring more nutrition, hydration, and accentuating any pedaling inefficiencies you might have.

Bike Fit

A correct bike fit is crucial to your ability to perform at your best on the bike leg of your race. More important even than owning a top-end expensive carbon race machine, a proper bike fit on whatever bike you are riding will not only make you more comfortable, but it will make you faster on and off the bike. A bike fit basically entails ensuring that you have the right size frame, the right seat height, and the most powerful fore and aft position for your seat, as well as cockpit considerations like stem length, aerobar height, and width for

Working on Your Pedal Stroke

While professional and highly proficient cyclists develop a smooth pedal stroke through years of riding long miles, drills are a time-effective way for a short-course triathlete to improve his or her cycling form without logging extreme mileage.

ONE-LEGGED DRILLS

This simple drill embeds neuromuscular pathways into your muscle memory by demanding that you work all the way through the pedal stroke. Perform it for 10 minutes at the beginning of your ride at least once per week for the best effect. To do the drill, unclip from the right pedal and pedal with only the left leg for 20 seconds. Shoot for a cadence of 60 rpms. Switch sides, and go back and forth for 20 seconds on each side. Build up to 10 sets of one minute on each leg for 20 minutes total. The goal of this drill is to "force out" the dead spots in your pedal stroke. You'll know it's working when you're pedaling at a high cadence without bouncing.

REFINING PEDALING SKILLS ON OTHER BIKES

A fixed gear bike forces you to pedal in circles, whether you want to or not. Imagine riding a spin bike—the kind that keeps pedaling even when you don't want to—out on the open road. This type of bike also helps athletes feel their way through the entire pedal stroke because when slowing down, you'll need to use the pedal stroke to help bring you to a stop if you choose to go brake-less. Just remember, the pedals never stop, so it's easy to get bucked off a fixed-gear bike or get injured if your experience level isn't high enough. For those with a less-adventurous spirit, mountain biking can also help develop a smooth, circular pedal stroke, along with better handling skills and increased strength development. If your pedal stroke isn't even while mountain biking, you will know it because your tires will slip out on loose surfaces. Also, uneven terrain helps for a more rhythmic, efficient pedal stroke. ▲

starters. An expert fitting can get into so much more. Time and time again we see 10-cent bike fits on $10,000 bikes—when the rider would have been better off purchasing a bike for half the price and spending some money on an expert bike fit. When looking for a good fitter, seek out someone who has experience fitting triathletes, as a tri fit is different from a road bike fit or even a time trial bike fit. From the greenest beginner to the most advanced professional, money spent on a good bike fit goes a long way to more productive training, faster racing, and even injury prevention.

Positioning on the Bike

The most important areas of comfort on a tri bike involve your "points of contact." Points of contact are the spots where you are physically touching the bike; if these spots are uncomfortable or don't place you in a powerful position, you are setting yourself up for a less-than-ideal bike ride right from the beginning. We discuss the various bike components that affect these points of contact in the gear section (see p. 33), but there are ways to physically connect with your bike that will help.

Seat

While almost any bike seat takes some getting used to and should be supplemented with a good pair of padded bike shorts, *how* your body perches on your (properly fitted) saddle is crucial. Position your sit bones—the hard parts under your body—on the saddle first, keeping your hips from rolling forward, initially. Once you find that proper sit-bone position, only then should you roll your shoulders—not your hips—forward to meet the handlebars with your hands. Always keep checking in to make sure that your hips haven't rolled too far forward, as that can place undue stress on the soft tissue of your delicate underparts, cause pain, and ultimately cause you to slow down as you shift around on the saddle and lift your body up while pedaling to alleviate the pressure.

Bars

A proper bike fit will help you get your cockpit (the term for the handlebars and aerobars) to the proper length, height, and width, but even once that's set up, it's important to "hold" your body on the bars in the correct way. As mentioned in Chapter 2, triathletes should seriously consider aerobars, as they provide not only extra speed—by lowering your body and compacting your elbows and shoulders to create a smaller footprint into the wind—but also a comfortable place to perch that "quiet" upper body we spoke about in the "Pedaling" section.

Envision your hands and elbows "resting" in the aerobars and your upper body "swinging" as in a hammock. Hold the aerobars as lightly as possible—while remaining in control—with your arms at a near 90-degree bend at the elbow. Shoulders should be dropped and rotated slightly inward (this can take time and practice for adequate flexibility), and your head should hang below your body. Imagine one string pulling your head forward and another string pulling your chin down. Be sure to keep your back gently rounded in order to keep a smooth line between the contact point on your seat and the contact point on your elbows. If you become too crunched, it can restrict your diaphragm and lungs.

Bike Handling: Descending and Cornering

Descending and cornering are often overlooked by triathletes who prefer to think of races as one straight line after another, but for short-course athletes, every second counts. You want to ensure that you are proficient in any type of course, maximizing your ability and skills along with your speed and strength. Not only that, but you may end up riding in a group situation during training or in a draft-legal race where you'll be in close proximity to other cyclists. Here is a top-down approach to handling your bike on descents and through corners that will also help ease any group-ride jitters:

HEAD AND EYES: As you approach a corner, be scanning for obstacles, such as bumps, off-camber sections, painted road, or anything else that might affect your "line" (the course you'll take through the corner). But remember that your eyes lead your head, which will in turn lead the rest of your body. Where the head goes, the body follows. Look where you *want* to go. All too often cyclists get tunnel vision on an obstacle or the outside or inside of a turn because that's where they are heading—sure enough, that's where they end up! So be intentional with your focus.

BODY: You might think that handlebars are what is steering your bike at speed. Think again. Sure, without them, we'd be stuck in a straight line (and probably fall over a lot), but your body is actually the thing that tells the bike where to go. You should be in your base bars (if you have aerobars) or the drops (if you have road bars)—from there, keep your weight low and forward. Think about weighting your bars via your shoulder toward the inside of the corner. More advanced descenders should approach a sharp turn at the outside of the corner, expecting to make their way toward the inside at the apex and exiting toward the outside again. Just remember to keep your upper body as low as possible for the safest and most predictable cornering.

BRAKING: Ideally, you wouldn't do any braking in the middle of a corner or descent, but this situation can arise. If braking in the middle of a corner (as opposed to before entering the corner, which is what you should be doing), rely on your back brake. While the front brake is your "power" brake, it can also cause you to lose control of your line as it forces your body to rise up, which is not ideal. Though it has less stopping power, the rear brake is more predictable through corners, provided you don't pull it so hard that you skid and lose traction. Only use the front brake in a corner if the rear brake isn't slowing you down fast enough to avoid an obstacle and you need to slow down quickly at the risk of coming out of the corner unpredictably.

LEGS AND FEET: As you approach the corner, be sure to raise the foot that will be on the inside to ensure a consistent line and—more importantly—to avoid scraping your pedal. If you're taking a right-hand turn, your right foot should come up, left foot down, with most of your lower body's weight on the left foot. However, still keep the weight of your upper body on your right hand in this situation. Keep your inside knee, the right knee in this example, pointed in the direction you want to go, and keep your right pedal up until you fully exit the corner or risk sliding out.

Descending and cornering require practice to help create muscle memory that can adapt to changing situations or unfamiliar courses. As often as you can, seek out a training course with a variety of challenging corners to work these essential skills, which when executed well, will provide you with free speed and reduced tension and energy expenditure on the bike.

RUNNING: BETTER FORM AND FUNCTION

Run technique has entire books devoted to it. We can't cover it as thoroughly as that here; however, what we can do is offer several key points that will absolutely help you build a stronger foundation and excel in the run portion of your race. In short-course racing, you want to exit the transition ready to run fast, as you won't have a lot of extra time to "find your stride." Aim to lock into good running form quickly in order to maximize every second on the course.

Part of the beauty of running is that it allows you time to think, as you are not as preoccupied with breathing and surviving (as in swimming) or staying safe and upright (as in cycling). This creates space to focus on running better. As in cycling, we'll approach our advice with a top-down strategy to get you closer to the running ideal. Consider the six points of assessment below, and focus on improving one aspect of your technique on every run.

Head

Many runners tend to look too far up or too far down, and it only gets worse with fatigue, wreaking havoc on your mechanics. Looking too far up can cause you to run too far back on your heels, and looking too far down can cause you to hunch over, losing your posture and the spring in your run. Fix your gaze 6 to 10 feet in front of you, and imagine someone pulling a string from the top of your head through your spine, like a puppet. Or, imagine trying to make the crown of your head touch an imaginary low ceiling. In other words, run tall.

Shoulders and Arms

Your arms drive your legs. If the arms don't move, then the legs won't move properly either. Focus on a linear arm swing; just as you wouldn't want your feet crossing in front of your body and tripping you up, you don't want your hands causing imbalance by crossing your body either. Imagine your shoulder as a pivot that allows your elbow (and hand) to swing straight forward and straight back only, nowhere else. Elbows should be at a 90-degree-or-less bend, swing freely, and be relaxed from your shoulders.

Hands

Relax your hands as you run; imagine holding an eggshell lightly between your thumb and pointer finger, firmly enough so it doesn't slip out, but not so tightly that you crush it. Keep focused on the rotation of your hands as well.

Oftentimes if your hands rotate outward, your feet will follow. Try to draw a straight line from your outer forearm to your hand's middle knuckle.

Torso and Hips

Proper running form starts with the hips because it is the hips that begin the chain of events that propels us forward. Unfortunately, as our daily jobs often involve lots of sitting, this can be the hardest place to improve upon. To run efficiently, work to shift the hips forward—underneath your body— rather than behind. This creates a "falling forward" effect that may feel a little like downhill running (and who doesn't love running downhill?). In this position, the foot should land directly under a slightly flexing knee, just ahead of the hips. The body will follow, shifting over the hips, helping the stride move behind the body and preventing overstriding.

Knees and Legs

Imagine your legs as whips, driven by your hips and glutes. Your foot should land directly under your knee—not ahead, as this creates overstriding and excessive heel striking—as your hip flows over your knee. Think of driving the knee forward on push-off in a perfectly straight line ahead. Your knees and back kick should both go higher as speed increases.

Feet

Feet are the tip of your body's running "whip." When the tip of the whip strikes the ground, imagine a powerful "crack" happening as you land on your forefoot. If you hit the ground with your heel instead, it will create a dull thud that not only indicates overstriding (which slows you down), but also creates a greater opportunity for injury. Similarly, you want that "crack" happening as quickly as possible. If you land on your heel, you have to roll all the way from your heel to the front of your foot before pushing off again; the longer you spend on the ground is more opportunity for your body to slow down. Aim to spend as little time on the ground as possible by landing on your forefoot. Toe-off happens at the front of the foot, so landing on the forefoot means less time from foot-strike to toe-off. Landing on the heel means you have to roll all the way from heel to toe, which takes more time.

You should aim for a cadence of about 180 foot strikes per minute (90 per foot). At slower paces, this means a shorter stride; at faster paces, this means an increased stride length, which is fine as long as you're still landing on your forefoot.

4

THE SUPPLEMENTARY WORK

The lighter mileage requirements for short-course triathlon mean that athletes have more time to do the extras that help prevent injury and make them not just fit triathletes, but more well-rounded athletes. Though we use the term "extra," in fact these supplementary sessions are truly essentials for success in short-course. Therefore, you need to approach these workouts and routines not as icing on the cake but rather as the glue that will hold everything together. Without that glue, your other training and racing can suffer, so it's important to treat these sessions with the same commitment and respect that you bring to your swim, bike, and run workouts.

NO MORE WEAK LINKS

Regularly swimming, biking, and running helps ensure that triathletes are generally well-balanced athletes doing a wide variety of movements. That variety in training not only keeps you motivated and excited to work out, but also goes a long way toward helping prevent injuries due to repetition. But it's also important to add intentional strength training into the mix both to help fill in any gaps that could cause injury and to improve sport-specific strength and power for your best short-course performances.

Though the short-course training plans in this book are aimed at three levels—newcomer, more experienced, and advanced—the strength training program is the same for all three. All triathletes, regardless of level, will benefit from increased strength and power as well as the injury prevention that supplementary training provides. That said, a few specific groups will benefit the most:

ATHLETES WITH CHRONIC INJURIES: Perhaps you've had a recurring injury in swimming, biking, or running, or maybe an injury developed in a different sport entirely. Either way, addressing weaknesses through strength training will position you to increase and intensify your training without injury coming back.

OLDER ATHLETES: As we age, injuries can become more commonplace. Along with a focus on dynamic stretching that we'll talk about later, athletes over age 50 should place particular emphasis on strength training to reduce possible imbalances and weaknesses that can lead to injury.

ATHLETES LACKING POWER OR STRENGTH: Many triathletes have one sport in which they are notably stronger while performance in the other two sports is relatively weaker. If you're more of a runner, you will see the benefits of strength training in your swimming and cycling; for swimmers, increased strength helps with power and injury prevention in your cycling and running; for cyclists, strength training will help prevent injury during running and much-needed upper-body power in the pool.

Multisport strength training is different from a regular strength training program. Though many of the movements may be the same, as triathletes, we

> Racing fast and having goals for my racing is important, but discipline is what I fall back on to get out the door—even when I do not want to.
>
> —2016 Olympian Ben Kanute

spend less time in the gym than someone who is not swimming, biking, and running because we are trying to maximize our time for short-course training. Studies have found that strength training one to two times per week is the sweet spot for triathletes. Twice per week is vastly superior to only going once, but going three times provides just marginal gains. Again, we are swimmers, bikers, and runners *first*—strength training, while crucial, is a means to supplement and enhance those three sports. Therefore, generally speaking, if life becomes too hectic and time becomes too much of a premium, strength training should be one of the first sessions to be skipped. However, if you recognize yourself in one of those "strength-crucial" categories listed, it's better to skip a recovery swim, bike, or run instead.

Strength Training

During each strength training session, you will perform the same exercises, but with variation in the amounts of weight, repetitions, sets, and recovery. It's important to do the exercises in the order listed, always alternating between lower- and upper-body movements, which allows one system to recover while working the other.

Athletes of all levels will perform the same movements for each strength session throughout the plan, although as the schedule progresses, the number of sets, the number of repetitions, the amount of weight, and the recovery time will change. The focus of the strength training sessions will also change, much like your swim, bike, and run workouts, as your training plan moves through phases. Regardless of weight, reps, or skill level, the most important

> Racing is my favorite part of the training cycle. I put in the hard work and love the grind of training because I get to taper and express it on race day.
>
> —2016 Olympian Ben Kanute

thing to keep in mind with strength training is your form. If form breaks down, the point of the strength workout has been lost.

For best results, consider scheduling a session with a personal trainer with the simple goal of learning each one of the movements perfectly. If that's not possible, online videos can also be a good resource.

While many of the movements for the strength training routine could be performed at home, you are better off going to a gym, if possible. Not only will a gym have the right equipment for the session, but there also can be a mental boost that comes from setting foot in a gym and putting yourself in the "strength training zone," helping you focus on the task at hand.

STRENGTH PROGRAM: THE KEY MOVEMENTS

Exercises in the strength program are illustrated here, with general instruction and key information about the role each has to play in your fitness. **You'll find the specific workout progressions in Appendix D.** It's important that you perform each movement properly.

LUNGES

HOW: Using dumbbells, let the weight hang at your sides, and step forward with one leg, keeping your back straight, shoulders proud, eyes ahead. Lunge down until your back knee is close to the ground.

WHY: Lunges are like the multisport athlete of strength training—they work the glutes, hamstrings, quadriceps, calves, abdominals, and back muscles. Great for swimming, biking, and running.

SHOULDER SHRUGS

HOW: With feet flat on the ground, shoulder-width apart, hold a bar (or barbell), letting the weight hang. Lean forward 10 degrees, bend the knees slightly, and shrug your shoulders up to your ears as high as possible. Pause at the top and slowly lower to repeat.

WHY: This versatile exercise works the upper trapezius muscles to stabilize and strengthen the neck and shoulders. Great for swimming, biking (particularly helpful for holding the head in the aero position), and running.

LEG PRESS

HOW: Position your feet shoulder-width apart and adjust any safety mechanism to release the weight. Extend the legs without locking the knees, pushing the weight through the heels as you exhale, and inhaling as the weight comes back toward you.

WHY: Leg presses create power in the glutes and quads. Due to the stability created by the leg press machine, you can feel free to add more weight, provided you maintain perfect form. Great for biking, especially those who struggle on the bike or are looking to add power.

BICEP CURL

HOW: Stand with feet shoulder-width apart, a dumbbell in each hand, with palms facing out. Keeping the elbows close and upper arms still, curl the weight upward as you exhale.

WHY: Curls strengthen triceps and shoulder muscles. Great for runners to improve arm swing.

DEAD LIFT

HOW: Grab the bar, squeeze your armpits, and lift your hips and shoulders simultaneously as one unit, with back flat—never rounded. Drive your feet into the floor and stand tall with hips pushed forward as you finish and slowly lower the bar. (Note: We recommend using a hex or trap bar for deadlifts. This will ensure maximum safety at all levels.)

WHY: Like lunges, deadlifts target multiple muscle groups, including hamstrings, quadriceps, lower back, and glutes. Great for improving strength and stability on the run and bike.

ROMAN CHAIR

HOW: This device will hold your lower body as you do a sit-up-type movement. The idea here is to work the hip flexor, so focus on using your hips to raise your upper body, not your abs. Keep your head, shoulders, and back in line, and don't let your shoulders roll forward.

WHY: As much as this movement helps build strength, it also goes a long way in preventing injury in an area that's notoriously weak for anyone who does a lot of sitting. Great for strengthening hip flexors on the bike and run.

SEATED HAMSTRING CURL

HOW: Placing the pad at the backs of the heels, breathe in, tense the hamstrings, and then curl the weight back and up toward the butt. Keep the back flat and spine straight—don't arch. Return to the starting position with control; don't let the weight stack drop. Keep your knees relaxed as you start to re-engage.

WHY: This exercise complements the glute and quad strength developed in the leg press motion with a focus on hamstrings. Great for running and building strength for the pull phase of a cycling pedal stroke.

LAT PULL-DOWN

HOW: Hold the bar slightly wider than shoulder width, with arms fully extended. Keeping your torso upright, tighten your core and focus on bringing your elbows—not your hands—down so that the bar hits your chest. Without breaking the line of your wrists, finish with a shoulder-blade squeeze.

WHY: This movement not only develops the latissimus dorsi muscles in the back, but also the shoulders and biceps. Great for improving muscular endurance for swimming.

LEG ABDUCTION/ADDUCTION

HOW: Using either a standing cable machine (not the seated version) or a stretch band, lift your outside leg from the anchor point away from the body out to the side, keeping the leg straight for abduction. For adduction, focus on pulling your leg across the centerline of your body, then pause briefly, and return to the starting position. Both movements are slow and controlled.

WHY: Because triathletes almost exclusively move with forward motion and very little lateral movement, it's important to work these muscles to prevent imbalances. Great for injury prevention, particularly on the run.

Core Routine

WHY: A tight core is the key to trunk stability, which can translate to injury prevention and better form, which then leads to increased efficiency. It's a chain reaction! All of the following abdominal exercises work in conjunction to prevent side-to-side "snaking" in the swim, holding a strong position on the bike, and improving trunk posture on the run.

CRUNCHES

HOW: With hands behind your head, rest your back flat on the floor, with knees bent and feet flat. Lift your chest up (without pulling on your neck), lower it back down, then repeat the movement rotating to one side, then a third time, rotating to the opposite side. Count this as 3 reps.

ELEVATED-LEG CRUNCHES

HOW: Perform this just like crunches, but with knees bent and raised, with feet facing the opposite wall. Keep abs activated at all times. Count the crunch up and to each side as 3 reps.

SIDE OBLIQUE CRUNCHES

HOW: With one hand behind your head, lie on one side with hips in a direct line, stacked one above the other, and crunch the upper shoulder toward the upper hip. Don't pull on your neck.

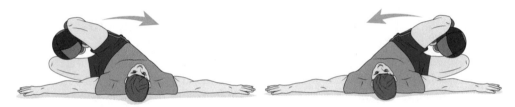

HIP ROLL

HOW: Lie on your back with knees raised and a medicine ball between them. With arms flat and straight out to the sides, slowly move from one side to the other, with control, while keeping the arms in contact with the ground. Start with a light weight.

LEG-EXTENSION CORE

HOW: Lie on your back with your hands at your sides. Extend your legs and point your toes, lifting your heels just off the ground. Bring your knees to starting position to create a 90-degree angle between your torso and your quads, and then extend them back.

Good Sore or Bad Sore?

While this book offers you a blueprint to get from day one to race day, remember, responsibility still falls on you, not only to do the workouts, but also to know when you need to take a day off. In the training plan intros, we'll discuss in detail how to adjust the plan (or not adjust it) if you take an unexpected day off, but just as importantly, you need to know when to dial it back during the plan itself. Regardless of your level of experience or even if you work with a coach, no one but you knows how your body feels on a given day.

We've all heard the old clichés—"Pain is temporary, victory is forever," or "What doesn't kill you makes you stronger"—but the truth of it is, those don't always hold up. Yes, sometimes pain really is simply "weakness leaving the body," and yes, some soreness is good, but other times pain is your body desperately trying to tell you something, like maybe "Stop!"

But how do we know the difference between a good hurt and a bad hurt; how do we know when a hurt is an injury?

Any time you begin a new exercise program—triathlon included—there will be soreness. Any time you start pushing your body harder than you have before, there will be soreness. Within this realm of hurt, there is muscular soreness (the good kind) and tendon or joint pain (the bad kind).

Good soreness has been associated with delayed onset muscle soreness (DOMS). Following a new or increased workload, you might experience muscle pain or weakness with symptoms that persist for a day or two. The more you work out and do similar sessions, the more your muscles will adapt to the workload and your DOMS will decrease. Expect to feel DOMS when you transition into different training phases or introduce new, faster workouts. Regarding the latter, you'll likely experience more DOMS as a short-course athlete than as a long-course one.

Bad soreness, on the other hand, is when you're on the road to developing an injury. If you're experiencing structural pain that lasts for more than a day or two (make a note in the plan to keep track), then it might well be time to take a day or two of rest. If the pain still hasn't subsided or—worse yet—the pain is causing your swim, bike, or run form to alter, or you're having to modify your daily nontriathlon activities, it might be time to see a professional. Some of the worst injuries can occur when we are trying to compensate for another injury. A small imbalance that causes you to limp on your left leg could then create a bigger injury to your right leg as you try to adjust.

Here we've broken down some common examples of "good" and "bad" soreness that you might experience during triathlon training. If you're experiencing the good kind, then this just might be "weakness leaving your body," but if you're feeling persistent "bad soreness," then the pain might not be temporary. Get it checked out before it gets worse and sidelines you for the season.

Swimming

GOOD SORE

▸ Weakness and discomfort in the shoulders causing an inability to lift arms above shoulder height

▸ Dull (not sharp) pain across the abdominals and abdomen

▸ Muscular pain in the area from the neck to the tops of the shoulders, likely as a result of head rotation during breathing

▸ Muscular tightness in the lats, pecs, and upper biceps, particularly common if using paddles or increased pulling

BAD SORE

▸ Sharp "pinpoint" pain in the shoulder joint, particularly in the front

▸ Clicking or popping in the shoulder, accompanied by sharp pain

▸ Reduced range of motion and pain in the cervical area from the neck to the middle of the back

▸ Numbness in the upper extremities or fingers »

Bike

GOOD SORE

▸ Muscular pain in the tops of the thighs, sometimes tender to the touch

▸ Lack of flexibility in the quads or glutes

▸ Lower back pain that is dull (not sharp)

▸ Tightness in the middle or upper back, particularly after long sessions spent in the aero position

BAD SORE

▸ Numbness or tingling in the hands

▸ Specific pain that limits range of motion in the knees

▸ Sharp lower-back pain with increased discomfort when standing or walking

▸ Pain in the front of the knee that gets worse when squatting or standing on one leg

Run

GOOD SORE

▸ Achy or sore calves that feel worse while walking or running up an incline

▸ Tightness in the side—the infamous side stitch—during a workout

▸ Mild tenderness under the ball of the foot during impact

▸ Mild tightness in the hamstrings while extending the leg

BAD SORE

▸ Knee or hip pain in the sides of either that can indicate iliotibial (IT) band issues, also known as "runner's knee"

▸ Specific pain in the Achilles tendon that is sore to the touch or during stretching, also weakness during heel raises

▸ Sharp pain under the ball of the foot

▸ Sharp pain on or in the shin bone ⚠

WARM IT UP, COOL IT DOWN

For any sport you participate in, a solid warm-up is an essential part of every workout. While you may think of it as optional, or even a waste of time, it's anything but. Imagine trying to drive a sports car (yes, this is your new short-course body!) as fast as it can go without letting the engine warm up. It might work for a little while, but the wear and tear on the inside of the engine will lead to poor performance—or even disaster—sooner or later. As many an athlete can attest, a lot of the minor injuries sustained during training and racing were a result of rushing, or eliminating, a proper warm-up.

Prime the Pump

In short-course training and racing, where you're often performing short, intense workouts, it's particularly important that your body be primed and ready when the "meat" of a workout begins. A well-crafted warm-up routine provides the body with **four major advantages** before a workout begins, allowing for peak performance during the workout, as well as going a long way toward preventing injury:

ACTIVATES THE NERVOUS SYSTEM: Warming up will quicken how fast signals move across the nerves. In swimming, this helps with getting a "feel" for the water; in cycling, you will be more effective at plugging in to your pedaling cycle (discussed in detail on pp. 54–55); and in running, you'll be able to better mimic the ideal form you're aiming for.

WARMS UP THE CARDIOVASCULAR SYSTEM: A proper warm-up helps increase the elasticity of the "balloon" that is your lungs, letting more oxygen fill that space and oxygenating the blood supply.

INCREASES BLOOD FLOW: This is the next step in the cardio chain. As more blood delivers more oxygen to more muscles, this is like the gasoline finally flowing to the pistons in the body's engine. In particular, increased blood flow to smaller stabilizer muscles helps ensure you don't get injured early in the workout.

RAISES BODY TEMPERATURE: By increasing your body's temperature, you're allowing your muscles and joints to have more free mobility—think of it as the oil flowing to the pistons, ensuring everything moves smoothly.

Sport-Specific Warm-Ups

Crucial for swimming, but also important for cycling and running, a sport-specific warm-up at the start of every workout will allow for the best possible conditions in each training session. As mentioned, a key advantage of focusing on short-course training and racing is that there's more time allotted for "extras" such as a proper warm-up—which of course isn't an "extra" at all. Remember, you need to squeeze a near-perfect workout out of almost every session, so be sure that your body is primed to perform when you call upon it. Building in a sound warm-up routine early in your training helps ensure that it becomes a daily habit—like tying your shoes—that you can't imagine beginning a workout without.

Every workout prescribed in this book begins with the warm-up prescribed below for each sport. For brick workouts (combination workouts such as swim-and-bike or bike-and-run), perform the warm-up indicated for the first sport in the brick.

Warming Up to Swim

Because swimming is so technique-driven and flexibility is crucial to good technique, it's wise to use a dynamic—or active—stretching program prior to the warm-up. Think of it like the warm-up's warm-up. It shouldn't take more than 5 to 10 minutes.

Dynamic Stretching Warm-Up

This routine consists of seven dynamic stretches designed to prepare you for an effective swim workout. Do each movement for about 20 seconds, performing the entire routine three times through.

TRIPLE EXTENSION Y-REACH

Squat down, keeping your knees behind your toes, and elongate your spine as you reach your hands up and forward. Extend hips, knees, and heels upward to create a straight line as you reach, placing your hands behind you, with your shoulders down.

CRAB HIP ROTATION

Rotate your hips so that all parts of the sides of your legs touch the ground, relaxing your lower back and stretching your hips. This is particularly useful if you've done a long ride or run prior to swimming. »

Continued

SIDE LYING WINDMILL

Start with hands together, lying on your side. Bring top hand above your face and past it until it hits the floor and opens your chest. Next, bring the moving arm in an arc above the top of your head, sweeping the floor if possible.

SHOULDER SHRUG OVERHEAD EXTENSION

Simply bring hands and shoulders up above your head while keeping all parts of your back touching the ground throughout the whole movement.

SCORPION

Lie on your stomach, hands to your sides with palms down. Twist your torso with a bent knee to have your left foot's toe touching your right hand. Halfway through the set, touch and hold the foot with the opposite hand.

IRON CROSS

Lift one foot with a locked knee as high as you can in front of you as you lie flat on your back with hands extended to sides, palms down. Move the foot in an arc above you to the opposite side of your body. When it touches the ground, sweep the leg across the ground beneath you to return to the starting position. Alternate legs.

PUSH-UP TO DOWNWARD DOG

Lie facedown on the ground, hands off the floor. Flex your scapula behind you, engage with your hands into a push-up as you bend into a pike, and use your shoulders to drive your heels backward. ▲

A dynamic warm-up will help your body prepare for what's coming in several key ways:

WAKES UP YOUR MUSCLES: A dynamic stretch will activate the muscles and prepare them for the swimming motions by increasing blood flow to neuro-muscular pathways.

INCREASES RANGE OF MOTION: The best swimmers in the world are highly flexible, allowing them to move efficiently through the water.

UPS THE "FEEL FACTOR": Body awareness, or a "feel" for the water, is key in good swimming. The better you can detect the water on your skin and muscles, the better you will be able to propel yourself through it.

MAXIMIZES YOUR PERFORMANCE: A smart, dynamic stretching routine will enhance muscular power and performance, making every stroke count, from warm-up to cooldown.

On the heels of your dynamic stretch routine, you will want to continue preparing the body for the upcoming main set. The swim workouts will specify a warm-up that includes a mix of easy swimming, drills, and maybe some short accelerations. Here's an example:

Swim Warm-Up

     200 easy swim, 30 sec. rest

     100 kick with kickboard or alignment board, 30 sec. rest

     200 pull with buoy, 30 sec. rest

     4 × 50 drill with 10 sec. rest

     4 × 50 descend within each 50, building to fast, with 15 sec. rest

     4 × 25 fast, with 30 rest

Warming Up to Bike

Although the warm-up routine outlined here is not essential to perform prior to aerobic rides in power or heart rate zones 1 or 2, it's still important to begin every ride with 10 to 15 minutes of light, zone 1 riding to prepare the body. To find out how to use power or heart rate zones to measure effort, see pp. 112–115. When doing intervals or harder tempo work, the following routine is absolutely necessary to ensure the set is performed properly and safely.

Bike Warm-Up

15–20 min. Z1/Z2

6 × 30–45 sec. spin-ups in a light gear, moving from a low cadence (60 rpm) to a high cadence (120+ rpm). The moment you begin to bounce in your seat, reduce cadence and spin easy for 2 min.

6 × 1 min. "primers" in Z4, with 2 min. recovery

Warming Up to Run

For light aerobic runs, a complete warm-up such as the one outlined below is not necessary. Instead, simply build into your run over the first 10 minutes. When doing higher intensity tempo or interval workouts, however, be sure to "prime" your body with a set similar to this.

Run Warm-Up

5–10 min. Z1

5 min. build to Z3

5 min. dynamic exercises or drills (see Appendix C, "Running Drills," p. 245)

6 × 60–75m strides at 80 percent of max speed effort, rest 90 sec. between intervals

Post-Workout Cooldown

While properly warming up is a key way to prime your muscles for an optimal workout—and it's *always* about quality over quantity in sprint training—a consistent cooldown is just as important to transition from working out to resting. Although studies are inconclusive that cooling down is effective for reducing muscle soreness, improving performance, or preventing injury, the process allows your heart rate, blood pressure, and respiration to return to a normal rate post-workout.

Two rules of thumb for a good cooldown are:

1. Do the same sport you were just performing.
2. Keep it between 5 and 15 minutes; the longer and more intense the workout, the longer the cooldown.

Make a solid cooldown a consistent part of your routine, signaling to your body that it's time to stop working and start resting and recovering.

5

THE STRATEGY

As if juggling swimming, biking, running weren't enough, there is yet another very important element that merits your focus in short-course tri: strategy. Strategy plays a greater role in short-course tri than in longer distances, as pre-race planning and quick decision-making skills aren't just going to get you to the finish, rather they can have a significant impact on your overall time, for better or worse. The good news is that strategy doesn't take a whole lot more *physical* effort to improve upon; it is about knowledge, practice, and mental focus on race day.

In this chapter we'll discuss the importance of planning ahead with race-day specificity, gaining as much knowledge as you can about your event, and executing a well-thought-out plan on the big day.

THE ART OF FORWARD THINKING

Although your race day may be months away, it's important to understand well in advance what that day will look like. Practicing race-day specificity means becoming familiar with the routines that you'll use the day before your race and on the day itself. The goal is to minimize surprises and create a comfortable routine that feels as automatic as tying your shoes.

Still, it's essential to remember one of the major rules of triathlon: Something will go wrong. With so many moving parts, so many sports, and so much equipment, the one thing you can count on is that not everything will go perfectly. If you can keep that in mind as you approach race day, you'll be more prepared to roll with the punches that will inevitably be thrown your way. In fact, by keeping with a routine and a set program, you'll be able to rely on the constants that you've practiced, even when things beyond your control occur.

The best thing to do with this chapter is read it through before you begin your training journey; then bookmark it and revisit it as you go along in your plan. Caution! Don't save this section for race week. Review it now and as you train, keeping these points in the back of your mind. Then reopen the chapter again on race week so that you feel comfortable with the routine as race day gets closer.

Race-Day Specificity

One of the main tenets underpinning this book is race-day specificity. This means training like you race in order to minimize surprises on race day and to physically and psychologically prepare the body and mind for the goal of this program: to race and to race well!

Race-day specificity is at work in all the plans and workouts in this book. In this chapter, we'll go over essential concepts that are specific to having the best race day possible, such as training the course, devising a plan, doing an effective race-day warm-up, and executing the perfect transition in your race when seconds count.

Train the Course

Surprises may be fun on your birthday, but they are decidedly *not* something you want on race day. In an ideal world, everything on race day would feel routine—almost boring—except for the effort you'll be putting out. In order to best prepare, take time to understand the specific features of the racecourse. While it's not always possible to actually swim, bike, and run on the course itself, you can still replicate certain unique aspects of a course that may not otherwise come up in day-to-day training. Most triathlons will post a course map online—learn what you can from the graphics, look online for race reports, or talk to local club members.

Since most triathlon swims take place in the open water, it's crucial to train in open water as much as possible. But it's useful to get even more specific in your training. If your race is in the ocean, try to train in the ocean. If it's in a river with currents, try to train in a river with similar currents. Almost all tri swims have buoys and tight turns; even if you don't have a buoy, you can still practice tight turns in the open water. If open water isn't an option for you, do your best to replicate these features in the pool. (For more on open-water technique, see pp. 50–53.)

When it comes to the bike, having the opportunity to ride the course before your event is a huge advantage, but it is not always possible. Even if you can't actually ride the course, you can work to understand the elevation profile of it. If it has hills, replicate those ascents and descents while training. Also, get a sense of the number of turns on the course. A course with many turns will affect the way you ride. Try to do some of your workouts on courses that have turns in awkward spots, such as in the middle of an interval. Your body needs to understand and practice how to decelerate into and accelerate out of those corners without putting too much stress on your legs.

RULES OF THE GAME

Though triathlon rules differ depending on what event and distance you're participating in, all triathletes should have a basic understanding of these key points:

▶ Generally, drafting in cycling—sitting immediately behind the person in front of you—is not allowed. The distance that must remain between cyclists varies, but it's generally somewhere between 20 and 35 feet.

▶ Wetsuits are allowed in water with a temperature of 78 degrees or less. Races will announce if an event is not wetsuit-legal.

▶ A helmet must be worn and buckled from the moment you touch your bike in T1 until you put your bike back in T2.

▶ Headphones are not allowed at any point during the race.

▶ You must provide everything you need. You can't take assistance from an outside source—for example, water or food—except from an official race volunteer.

▶ You cannot throw trash along the course. Put gel and bar wrappers in a jersey pocket or bento box.

These are the bare minimum rules, and most races will have additional rules that involve where and when a race number must be worn, what type of clothing is allowed, and more. Violating any of these rules can result in a time penalty, or worse, a disqualification. Be sure to check rules on the race's website.

The advice for the bike course also applies to the run course. You will want to understand the elevation profile and simulate any hills in your workouts. It's also key to do training workouts on a course with similar turns, or lack thereof. While being able to decelerate and accelerate around tight turns—or U-turns around cones—is important, it's also important to get used to running long, straight stretches while maintaining your mental and physical intensity. Those long stretches should be practiced in training, otherwise they can be deadly to a successful run leg.

The Taper: Trust Don't Test

Leading up to race week, if you've followed the taper set out in the plan, you will be feeling fresh, fast, and powerful. Resist the urge to use this extra energy to build confidence by doing your workouts faster than normal. The idea of a smart taper is to bank the extra energy that you'll feel with a reduced workload. Continuously ask yourself, "Could I go harder if I needed to?" If the answer is *no*, then you need to back off.

There will be workouts where we try to measure progress, create benchmarks, and build confidence, but race week is not the appropriate time. You'll get your chance to prove your fitness on race day. Meanwhile, trust that the work you've done over the last several weeks will make you ready for your best possible day when the gun goes off. The reality is that at this point, if you're not ready, there's nothing you can do to prepare except rest anyway; there's not room to build fitness on race week.

Race-Day Warm-Up

It's important to have a set warm-up routine that prepares you for race morning, one that is familiar and repeatable. This is as much for *mental* preparation as it is for physical. If you can do the same race-day warm-up over and over again, your body and mind will fall into a recognizable pattern that places you in a familiar "ready state," signaling your body to slightly relax. We've provided a routine that you can use on the morning of your event, as well as occasionally for brick workouts; every athlete is different, so you may want to tweak the routine to get more of what you need. Ideally, begin this warm-up one hour before the start of your wave, in the order listed:

Bike

Starting your warm-up on the bike is usually a logistical necessity as you'll need to rack the bike in the transition area well before the start of the race. This also gives you the opportunity to test your bike and do any last-minute adjustments if there are any issues.

The warm-up ▸ 8 to 10 minutes aerobic riding with 4 × 30 seconds of accelerations at race pace with 1 minute of spinning between each. Run through all the gears, check both brakes, and take some corners at speed to give a thorough pre-race check while warming up.

Run

Immediately after biking, grab your running shoes and head out. Don't worry about setting up transition completely, just place your gear near your racked bike and run.

The warm-up ▸ 5 to 8 minutes in zone 1 with 4 × 20-second accelerations to race pace with 1:10 of easy jogging between each. Finish with a light stretch, and head back to transition to finish setting up.

Swim

Complete your transition area setup; then grab what you need to start the race and head to the swim start. Time this so that you'll have 15 to 20 minutes before the start of your wave. Bear in mind, there may be other waves going off, so be aware and ready to adapt.

The warm-up ▸ Swim for 6 to 10 minutes in full race-ready gear (wetsuit, race suit, cap, goggles) with 4 × 30-second accelerations at race pace with one minute of easy swimming between each.

Dynamic Exercises

These are not essential but are a useful way to fill the time between the end of the warm-up and the start of the race. It's important that you don't start the race with a low heart rate.

The warm-up ▸ Do as much (or as little) of the "Dynamic Stretching Warm-Up" routine (see pp. 81–83) to fill the time until the start of your wave. You may see other people resting and even lying down, but this is not the best thing to do. A slightly elevated heart rate and warm muscles are more advantageous than a few minutes of rest!

Expect the Unexpected on Race Day

Just as athletes are all different, so too are racecourses, so a warm-up on one course might not work on another. When thrown a warm-up curveball, here are some useful ways to respond:

⚠️ **No water access before the start**
Due to logistics or unpredictable conditions, race organizers sometimes won't let athletes warm up in the water. If this is the case, just remind yourself that everyone is in the same boat, so no one has an advantage here—except the people who remain calm and adapt. You can instead:

- ▸ Bring swim bands for a dryland warm-up, if you're comfortable using them. However, don't do anything new on race day.
- ▸ Do the "Dynamic Stretching Warm-Up" routine (see pp. 81–83). These familiar movements will get you very close to ready.

▶ Add additional running and/or biking to your warm-up, and do it a little closer to race time.

⚠ Roads closed to cyclists or unsafe riding before the start

This is common. If you have already researched the course, as suggested earlier in this chapter, this should come as no surprise. Be prepared:

▶ Set up a trainer in the transition area. This allows you to do a familiar bike warm-up and also ensures you don't have to worry about flats or unfamiliar areas right before your race.

▶ If you can't bring a trainer, extend your run and swim warm-ups, but still be sure to run through your gears and check your brakes before racking your bike. A big part of the bike warm-up is about making sure everything works well.

⚠ Transition area closes way before the start

This is common at large races or if you are in a later swim wave. Not having access to the transition area an hour or more before the start of your race simply means a little more foresight is needed:

▶ Bring an extra pair of running shoes and clothes. Since your bike will be "locked up" early, you'll focus instead on your swim and/or run warm-up. But since your run gear is "locked" in transition, as well, you'll need duplicate gear for your run warm-up. A set of clothes for warm-up that you then change out of and into a dry race kit goes a long way to keeping warm prior to the race start.

▶ If you need to change the order of your warm-up routine, that's perfectly fine. But one rule stands firm: Don't warm up more than an hour before your start time. That may mean getting creative, but if you brought enough equipment, it shouldn't be a problem.

DEVISING YOUR GAME PLAN

One thing that makes short-course triathlon especially exciting is that you get a chance to try different approaches that can drastically affect the outcome of your race. Even better, if they don't work out, you can try again, as soon as the next transition! Approaching a race with multiple mindsets can do almost as much as lots of extra training.

In this section, we'll address the outlooks and approaches you might apply to each of the three sports in short-course triathlon. Even if you're an experienced swimmer, biker, or runner, a winning strategy for triathlon is very different from how you'd approach a single-sport event. In multisport competition, you need to complete three very different sports and you'll very likely be arriving at the start of each sport fatigued. Every transition provides you with a chance to regroup and apply a new strategy, and if practiced properly, you can fall back on these strategies as you begin to tire.

Similarly, going in with a specific game plan—whether it be visualization, a mantra, or a goal—will help you remain in control when things start to go sideways. Take a look at the strategies below, pull out what you think will be important based on your goals, and remind yourself to "activate" that strategy during the race. A strategy isn't any good if you lose it in the fog of race day.

While a mantra—a simple phrase you prepare for each leg and before the start of the race—is good, even better is putting a meaningful word or phrase somewhere you can see it. It could be something like "Don't race" written on a piece of paper on your bike's top tube to act as a signal to stay within yourself. Or "Get ready to hurt" written in a black sharpie on a gel you'll take right before T2. Be creative and personal. These tips will ring a bell when you really need them.

Goals vary, so we've broken our mental tips and race strategies into two levels: Beginner is for a newer athlete with a goal that centers more around just finishing, and advanced is for the veteran athlete with a competitive eye to upping his or her game.

Overall Approach

BEGINNER: Think of race day as more an *experience* than as a race. Remember, the only guarantee is that despite well-laid plans and smart strategizing, something unexpected *will* happen. Don't let those moments derail you; rather view them as a learning experience. If you don't expect everything to go perfectly to plan, you won't be disappointed when it doesn't.

ADVANCED: Your overarching aim is to race better and faster, either than you have before, or than the competition. Your top-level approach should be a mixture of finding a pace that you know you can hold and handle and competing with those around you. Overdoing it a little is sometimes the best way to find your limits, even if risky, and you can always race again fairly soon.

Swim Strategy

BEGINNER: Before the race begins, take a few minutes to visualize swimming with other people around you, and no matter what speed you start at when the gun goes off, back it down a notch or two for the first few minutes. It's easier to build into a harder pace and find a higher heart rate than it is to back down your heart rate, effort, or pace if you go out too hard. Think of it this way: A swim start that's too fast can take a long time to recover from; a swim start that's too slow can be adjusted immediately.

ADVANCED: The swim is very important in short-course racing, more so than in long-course, because it sets you up for success later by putting you in a competitive group. It's key to find someone a little faster than you and stick to their feet. When the gun goes off, back off your pace by a notch or two, and find someone who is swimming past you slowly, not flying past. Position yourself on his or her feet at a pace that feels manageable for at least 20 to 30 minutes. If you can't imagine holding the pace for more than a few minutes, then you're going too fast.

Bike Strategy

BEGINNER: Prior to the race, and while training, visualize what it will be like to hold a steady, even pace and cadence throughout the entire bike leg, regardless of what's happening around you, and then execute on that. It can be easy on the bike to respond to other racers and try to "race" early in the event. If that happens, remind yourself that this is an *experience* more than a race, and you're trying to understand the sport and what you can do. Avoid succumbing to emotions when getting passed. Ignore it and stick to your pace, saving the heroics for another race or late in the run.

ADVANCED: A quick transition to the bike leg is crucial as it will either boost you into a group that's as fast or faster than you or it will put you behind. Be as competitive in your transition as you are with every other leg in the race. Move quickly and decisively, getting into your bike shoes on the go and doing your best to catch the next person in front of you. An early carrot can be invaluable to help push your pace in the middle of the bike. If you respond to people passing you, do it over a period of 30 seconds, not instantly. You want to push yourself on the bike because it'll do less damage than pushing yourself on the run.

Run Strategy

BEGINNER: The run can come as a shock for everyone, from beginners to experienced triathletes. A little too much effort on the swim or—more likely—on the bike can add up when coming out of T2. The best way to prepare yourself for the run is to expect that it will feel worse and be harder than you are used to. This way when you head out on the run and your legs feel like jelly, you're not caught by surprise. It's possible your legs will feel worse than they have in training, but remind yourself that this is only because you're pushing yourself harder on race day than you did in workouts. Instead of worrying, control what you can control: Focus on your form and stay positive. Rather than thinking about your pace, your splits, or your finishing time, create small goals for yourself (*"I'll run 20 great steps at this pace, then go easier for 6 steps"*).

ADVANCED: Near the end of the bike—think final two minutes—take the opportunity to loosen up your legs, lower your gear, spin, and mentally prepare yourself for T2. It's okay to lose a little bit of competitive fire near the end of the bike and let a few cyclists go—a minute of easy riding here will pay off with a better run split later, hence why it's mentioned here in the run section. Don't rush T2 quite as much as T1 because you won't be able to fix things like you could while riding your bike. Your legs may not feel great off the bike—be prepared for that and look forward to them coming around 5 or 10 minutes into the run. Remind yourself that you've done the training and have faith that you're physically ready, all the while knowing that you may need to push yourself *mentally* when it gets really tough. If you're struggling, think about small goals (*"I'll push this next hill, and then 'float' the downhill,"* or *"I'll run hard for 40 steps, then easy for 10"*) and not how much more you have ahead, but that you *only* have so many minutes to pass as many people (or gain as much ground) as possible. In the last half mile, turn off all pacing and focus on "emptying the tank" and giving everything you have left. You should hit the finish line completely spent.

TRANSITIONS

When triathletes shift from swim to bike and bike to run, they do so in an appointed spot on the course known as the transition area. You may not think transitions are particularly important, but for short-course racing, they are an essential skill that is almost as crucial as knowing how to properly pedal your bike or sight in the open water.

I know from personal experience the effect that a poor transition can have on your race. When I was racing for the US national team, I was not a strong swimmer. This meant that there were times when I would not be in the lead group coming out of the water, and therefore not in the lead group on the bike. Often I would spend the first half of the bike leg (or sometimes the whole thing) catching the 10–15 triathletes who would eventually make up the top 10–15 runners at the end of the day. Sometimes I could make it up on the run, but not always.

In 2010, I was at the ITU World Championship Series in Hamburg, Germany. I had flown over from my home in the US, trained there for a week, and was ready to go. The gun went off, and I had a decent swim, just behind the main group. But unfortunately, I didn't have a good transition—I struggled putting on my helmet, but didn't think it was a big deal in the moment. I figured I could make up for it. To this day, I remember the bike pack of almost 50 men riding away from me on the narrow, bumpy streets of Hamburg as I fumbled with my shoes on my bike. I never caught them and ended up a disastrous 49th place—almost last—returning to the US the next day with nothing to show for it.

In short-course, your transition can have a dramatic effect and can mean getting in with a group that will pull you along on the bike or being left behind. Because short-course racing—especially sprint-distance—is so quick, there's often very little time to make up any ground you lose. Every second counts.

Transition 101

Setup

Do not underestimate the value of a proper setup in the transition area. The key is being consistent and keeping it to the essentials. Furthermore, everything should be arranged in a familiar and orderly fashion before the gun goes off, so be sure to leave lots of extra time to set up your transition area on race morning.

My own list of items needed for transitions is sparse, in order to keep clutter at bay and decision-making to a minimum. You will want to make your own list based on what you feel you need, but it should include no more than 12 items (see Tables 5.1 and 5.2).

That may not seem like much gear, but that's the point. Anything else you need you can either get on the course, such as additional water from aid stations—or you should take care of prior to race start, such as (waterproof) sunscreen. Short-course racing is all about speed, and all that extra stuff just gets in the way and clutters what should be a simple and clean transition area. It's not a place to be waffling over decisions about whether to wear the visor or baseball cap, or if you want to wear socks. All of that should be well-thought-out beforehand, and other equipment outside of those necessities should be stored in a bag that is neatly tucked away from your bike rack to prevent clutter. If there are nonessential emergency items you think you might need, keep those near the top of your bag, just in case.

Order of Operations

Remember in algebra class where we learned about the order of operations for what came first when doing a complicated math problem? Parenthesis first, then multiplication, then addition, and so on. Transitions have an order of operations, too, and they are almost as strict. By sticking to this recommended order, you'll have a process that's familiar and repeatable—no matter what else is happening around you or to you in the race.

TABLE 5.1. T1 (Swim to Bike)

GEAR	POSITION
Helmet	Hanging on bike
Sunglasses	Hanging (securely!) on bike
Nutrition	In bento box on bike or taped to top tube
Hydration	In bottles and attached to bike
Bike shoes	Attached to pedals (with rubber bands going from heel to bike frame to keep heels from skidding and spinning while running), and open with powder inside to ease putting them on
Bike	In an easy gear, hung by bars or seat, both pedals at three o'clock
Number belt (if required on bike)	Hanging from seat

TABLE 5.2. T2 (Bike to Run)

GEAR	POSITION
Running shoes	Laces open, tongue pulled back, with powder inside to ease putting them on
Number belt (if not required on bike)	In a ball with your hat (if desired) or next to shoes
Hat (if desired)	Behind shoes
Sunglasses	Behind shoes (if different than cycling pair)
Nutrition	Pre-attached to number belt or inside belt pocket. These can also be stored in race suit pockets.

Set aside five minutes to run or walk the most direct route from the swim exit to your spot at the bike rack. Don't leave this to the last minute—it is as important as making sure all of your gear is in place. Rehearse the route at least twice from swim exit to bike rack spot, from bike rack spot to bike exit, from bike entry to bike rack spot, and from bike rack spot to run exit. This is a requirement for a short-course athlete of any level.

Here are some more valuable on-the-ground tips and tricks to help you set up your own order of operations.

T1 (Swim to Bike)

1. As you exit the water, loosen the neck of your wetsuit, unzip the back, and pull it off your shoulders and arms. If you start this process the *second* you stand up out of the water, you'll save precious time wrestling with the wetsuit as you run to the transition area. (Pre-race lube helps with this removal, see p. 30.)

2. With your wetsuit at your waist, run toward T1, removing cap and goggles and holding them in one hand so you can toss them together when you get to your spot.

3. Once at your T1 spot, drop your cap and goggles, put on your helmet, and *connect the strap.* Yes, your wetsuit still needs to come off, but the helmet strap is easy to forget and not having it fastened properly coming out of T1 can earn you a costly penalty.

4. Peel off your wetsuit by pulling the wetsuit legs as far down as you can, rolling the suit to become inside out. If you have to sit down to remove the legs from your feet (the hardest part), do so. Slide your fingers between your ankles or heels and the wetsuit opening to free the rubber from your heel area. Practice this many times before race day—it's a fine art.

5. Either put on your bike shoes and run or walk with your bike to the bike course start or grab your bike and run barefoot to the bike course start, where you'll put on your shoes and tighten them as you're riding. For advanced athletes who have practiced this before race day, keep your shoes clipped into the pedals and run with the shoes—rubber-banded to your bike to keep horizontal— attached to the bike. You'll do a "flying mount" (see p. 105) after passing the mount line, pedal up to near full-speed, and *then* slide your feet into the open holes of your shoes. Take a few more pedals to regain speed; then tighten the shoes down. For newer triathletes, put on your shoes and head to the bike exit.

Cycling shoes can be slippery, so walk if you must—saving a few seconds by running isn't worth sliding, falling, and hurting yourself or someone else. Regardless, be sure to mount your bike *after* the mount line.

6. Once on the course, double-check that your brakes are still centered in the front and rear. Better to stop early on to fix them than to have an energy-sapping brake issue for most of your bike leg. Also, now is the time to put on your sunglasses and take in nutrition, if desired.

T2 (Bike to Run)

1. As you come in off the bike, keep an eye out for the dismount line. Getting off your bike *after* the dismount line will earn you a hefty penalty, and many races have judges at the line watching for that mistake; it's an easy one to make.

2. Less-experienced riders should stop before the dismount line, unclip, then run or walk to the bike rack. Those with more experience can get their feet out of their shoes in the final 400 meters of the bike, and hop off barefoot before the dismount line.

3. At the rack, hang your bike by the bars or the seat, depending on the size of the rack and the size of the bike. Put your running shoes on, then remove your helmet, and place it on your bike. Your shoes should be equipped with open speed laces (see p. 40), filled with foot powder, and pulled open. For short-course, socks are rarely needed on the run. We're all about speed, and fussing with socks on wet feet not only takes time, but it also complicates a simple transition process.

4. Grab hat and race number belt in hand and go! As you exit T2, put on your hat, fasten your race belt, and take in any nutrition you want as you're running.

Practice Makes Perfect

There's no way to overstate the importance of transitions in short-course racing. When every second counts, you simply must maximize every moment
toward going faster and getting better. Therefore, you must be training your
transitions, alongside your workouts. We've built transition practice sessions
into the programs because it's that important to getting what is effectively
"free speed" on race day. The motions should feel absolutely automatic, like
signing your name, so you could do them with your eyes closed.

The Flying Mount

With practice, almost anyone can do some version of this time-saving maneuver. The first dozen times you attempt the flying mount, you should be practicing in an empty parking lot or driveway, free from vehicles or other people. Set aside 30 minutes to get the hang of the following steps:

1. Put your bike into an easy gear, one you'd feel comfortable starting in from a stop.

2. Put on your cycling shoes, stand above your bike and clip in the left foot. Open the left shoe and take your foot out, leaving the shoe to dangle, still connected to the pedal. Do the same for the right foot.

3. Once both shoes are clipped in, pull the tongue and sides of the shoe's upper to make the opening for your foot as wide as possible. Tri-specific shoes may have a strap with a notch to keep it open wide or some other kind of feature to keep the shoe very open.

4. Attach a thin rubber band from the heel of the right shoe, positioned at three o'clock, to your front derailleur. Tri-specific shoes will have a tab; regular road shoes may need to have two small cuts made in the outside of the heel fabric. Do the same for the left shoe but attach the rubber band from the heel to your left rear skewer.

5. With the shoes now horizontal and open, they shouldn't drag on the ground. It's important that you use a rubber band that is strong enough to hold the shoes in this position as you run with your bike, but that will break once you start pedaling. I've seen people pedaling miles into a bike course with a rubber band still tugging on their shoes.

6. Lean your bike against a wall or car—make it as similar to a transition area as possible. »

7. Run toward the bike, and grab it with one hand on the bars, one hand on the seat, bike to your right side. Run for at least 30 feet, getting the hang of how it moves next to you and how to steer clear of the dangling shoes, all while making sure the handlebars don't dance around. Eventually you might feel more comfortable just grabbing it by the seat.

8. At a preset "mount line," try one of the two methods below. The easier is first; a more advanced version is second:

Slow down slightly from a run, grab the bars with both hands, and step down on the left shoe—likely breaking the rubber band. You should still be coasting forward with your right foot slightly behind you, clear of the spokes in the rear wheel. Swing your right leg *behind* the seat, onto the right shoe, and sit down.

Maintaining your running speed, grab the bars with both hands, and jump up *and forward* with both feet. In the air, straighten your right leg and swing it behind the seat, over the rear wheel. The goal is to land with the inside of your left thigh on the seat *before* putting your feet onto your open shoes. Note: The more confident you are with this move, the easier it is. The more tenuous and slowly you do it, the harder it is to get over the rear wheel and hit the thigh target on the seat.

9. Once your feet are on top of your shoes and you're seated on the bike, start pedaling and get close to race speed. Only then should you try to get your feet, one at a time, into your shoes. Get the right foot in, pedal to regain speed, then get your left foot in. Pedal again to get up to full speed once both feet are inside the shoes (use a tri-specific shoe's heel tab to help), then—finally—tighten down the straps.

This method should be practiced many times before attempting on a racecourse, as doing the mount improperly can cause a lot of swerving that could be dangerous to other riders. ▲

YOUR
16-WEEK
PROGRAMS

6

INTRODUCTION TO THE TRAINING PLANS

In the following chapters, you'll find three training programs to choose from. For those of you who are brand-new to the sport, turn to p. 123 for the Level 1 Program. For those who have competed in a handful of triathlon events and would like to step up from simply crossing the finish line to finishing better, turn to p. 161 for the Level 2 Program. For seasoned triathletes who have been in the sport a while (whether in short distances or long distances) and are looking to squeeze everything they can out of short-course racing, check out the Level 3 performance program on p. 197.

If you're not sure about moving up in levels but want to learn more about training, there is plenty of valuable information in the higher-level plans that has been left out of Level 1 for the sake of simplicity. So even if you're not quite ready to take the next step, it's worth skimming the Level 2 and Level 3 introductions and plans for a deeper dive into training science. The higher-level training plans not only have more advanced training techniques, but they also will require more time and energy. The paces become more precise and sometimes require more equipment in order to train as accurately as possible.

On the other hand, there is some information that all levels of triathletes need to know in order to execute their best race. Familiarize yourself with the terminology and workout key below in order to train with purpose and use the plans in the pages that follow.

TRAINING PHASES

We'll cover the phases in-depth as you make your way through your plan, but at the onset, it's important to understand what you'll be experiencing as you make your way through the next 16 weeks.

PHASE 1 PREP AND ADAPTATION (TWO WEEKS): For Level 1, this phase begins to teach your body what it's like to train as a triathlete. In Level 2, this phase accommodates for a body that hasn't recently been training. Meanwhile, this phase in the Level 3 Program has a much sharper "slope" when going from no activity to full training.

PHASE 2 BASE (SIX WEEKS): The base phase is key, as you will need to build a substantial foundation to accommodate the intense build phase to come. The volume of training increases with each level.

PHASE 3 BUILD (SIX WEEKS): This phase focuses on intensity, with volume remaining highest in Level 3. Across all levels, it's important to focus on proper recovery during this phase.

PHASE 4 PEAK (TWO WEEKS): This phase guides you as you back down in volume while maintaining some intensity to taper and prepare for race day. Especially in the more competitive Level 2 and 3 plans, this is the time to really focus on your mindset.

MEASURING EFFORT

There are many different ways to gauge how much effort you need to put into each workout. For Level 1 and 2 athletes (and Level 3 athletes without a power meter), you can use rate of perceived exertion (RPE) or heart rate tests to figure out your specific heart zones. Level 3 athletes can measure effort by RPE, pace, and power. **The tests and the calculations to determine your zones for heart rate, pace, and power can all be found in Appendix A.** Each workout will give you guidance on effort and intensity.

Rate of Perceived Exertion (RPE)

RPE is a subjective unit of measurement that is particularly popular with beginners or triathletes who prefer to train low-tech. When overlaid with objective measurements, RPE can be a very powerful tool. Beginners can use RPE to train without the need for expensive equipment or tests, and advanced triathletes can use RPE to free themselves from the restraints of numbers and "race by feel."

TABLE 6.1. RPE Scale

RATING	INTENSITY/EFFORT	DESCRIPTION
0	Complete rest	Lying down, relaxing.
1	Very easy	Mostly inactive, i.e., standing or brief walking.
2	Easy	Comfortably walking. Can easily hold a conversation.
3	Easy to moderate	Brisk walking or movement. Can still hold a conversation.
4	Moderate	Aerobic effort. Breath is starting to be labored.
5	Moderate to hard	Manageable aerobic effort with increasing intensity.
6	Hard	More vigorous effort with increasing discomfort. Hard to get out more than a few words.
7	Harder	Vigorous, uncomfortable effort, with little to no talking.
8	Really hard	Strenuous exercise that can't be sustained very long.
9	Really, really hard	Very strenuous exercise lasting 1 minute, max.
10	All-out	Maximum effort pushing the limits, very short in duration.

Heart Rate

Another way that exertion is measured is by heart rate. Heart rate is one of the oldest modern measurements of physiological effort. It has been used for around 50 years in both lab and practical settings; therefore, it has a well-tested background and a long history of success with a scale based on percentages of maximum heart rate or lactate threshold heart rate.

Heart rate zones can vary widely based on age, gender, natural physiology, and fitness level. Each person's heart rate zones can also vary based on his or her daily condition as well as increasing (or decreasing) fitness. With that in mind, it's important to retest heart rate zones at least every eight weeks.

In order to determine the correct training zones that are used in this book, we recommend doing a max heart rate test or a lactate threshold test to get accurate results, both of which are found in Appendix A. Though a generalized "max-heart-rate-minus-age" test is popular and easy, this is definitely not accurate enough for triathlon training purposes and certainly won't reflect an individual's changing fitness as it progresses during the season. If you are a Level 1 athlete, **use the Run Max Heart Rate (MHR) Test on p. 236 to determine both running and cycling heart rate zones.**

The Lactate Threshold Heart Rate Test (LTHR)

LTHR is another great test to determine heart rate zones for cycling and running. **Use the tests on pp. 235–236 if you are a Level 2 athlete or Level 3 without a power meter.** We use the zones developed by coach Joe Friel, and

> You can determine cycling heart rate zones from running heart rate zones by using the MHR Test run zones in Appendix A and subtracting 10 beats per minute from the run test max. If you come from a cycling background or are a very experienced cyclist, you can use the same heart rate zones for cycling and running.

ZONE REFERENCE 101

		SYSTEM	MAX HEART RATE
ZONE 1	▶	Aerobic/Recovery	<74%
ZONE 2	▶	Endurance	74–79%
ZONE 3	▶	Intensive Endurance	80–83%
ZONE 4	▶	Sub-Threshold	84–89%
ZONE 5			
A	▶	Threshold	90–93%
B	▶	Anaerobic Endurance	94–97%
C	▶	Power	98–100%

these tests are the best way to determine objective efforts of measurement on your own. For the most accurate training zones, however, you can hire an endurance sports physiologist to determine very specific training zones in a lab setting with a bike ergometer for cycling and a treadmill for running. Just remember, it's important to remeasure these zones every eight weeks to keep your training accurate and on track.

Pace Zones

Best used for swimming and running, pace zones—like minutes per 100 yards for swimming or minutes per mile for running—need to be used in conjunction with heart rate or RPE. Level 3 athletes should use pace zones to track training or for hitting specific race time goals, and they need to be retested every six to eight weeks, just like heart rate zones.

When using pace zones for swimming, be certain of the pool length (yards or meters; 25, 33, or 50) and know that open-water pace zones are only accurate with a physical measured length. GPS watches are notoriously inaccurate in open water, and factors such as tides, currents, and waves play a big role in pace variations. **Complete the Swim Threshold Pace (STP) test on p. 234 to determine your pace zones for swimming.**

When using pace zones for running, a track or measured (and uninterrupted) repeatable distance is the best environment. Though fine for most situations, a GPS watch can still be inconsistent when measuring distances for pacing—particularly for short intervals. Other factors such as terrain, turns, and weather can also play a role in pace variations. **Complete the Run Threshold Pace (RTP) test on p. 237 to determine your pace zones for running.**

Power

Power is one of the most objective and easily correlated ways of measuring effort. As power meters have become less expensive—and have worked their way from simply cycling to cycling and running (and even swimming as well)—more triathletes are using power to train. Power can be used to set up training zones, monitor progress, and even set up racing plans.

Because it is consistent and produces the same results regardless of internal conditions—such as physiological factors that can affect heart rate, or external conditions, like terrain or environment that can affect pace—power is effort measurement at its most distilled. For the best use of Level 3 athletes' short-course training time, we strongly recommend purchasing a power meter that is consistent, reliable, and usable for all of your cycling (or running) needs.

Though much newer than cycling power, running power is a very valuable tool to measure effort. However, running power is quite different from cycling power and requires a different mindset. In cycling power, we're generally looking for higher power over a greater time (at a lower heart rate) because higher power in cycling equates to speed. In running, we're looking for a higher speed at a lower power—more efficiency—because higher power does not always mean higher speed. We want to generate the lowest power number while running as fast as possible. Of course, the faster you run, the higher the power number, so running with power also shows effort as well. It's important to generate more power (and run faster) for longer periods of time. Your aim is to become more efficient (less power at a similar speed) and more powerful (over a longer distance), a balancing act that is very different from cycling with power.

To find your cycling power zones, use the Bike Functional Threshold Power (FTP) test on p. 234. Technically, FTP is the average power for an hour time trial, but in practice it can be difficult to perform a consistent test of this length while training often. To get the most accurate power zones, it's important to do this abbreviated test *outside* on an open length of flat, uninterrupted road. Keep in mind that there are a few methods of determining FTP, but for the purposes of this book, we'll use a relatively simple test that is easily repeatable throughout the season.

To find your running power zones, use the Run Functional Threshold Power (RFTP) test on p. 238. To get the most accurate power zones, it's best to do this test on a measured track in normal training conditions (no unusually high or low temperatures, wind, or rain), but flat, uninterrupted road works well too. You will need a GPS smartwatch that is capable of measuring distance, heart rate, and power from the watch or shoe-mounted sensor.

THE KEY

The following workout descriptions will guide you through the day-to-day rhythm of the training program and arm you with knowledge of the purpose of each workout. In Table 6.2 you can see how this work fits into the four phases of your 16-week program. The notations and heart rate zones are the same for all plans; power zones are for Level 3 athletes. Specifics of each individual workout are referred to in the plan itself with Strength Training routines in Appendix D (pp. 251–255).

Key to Workouts & Intervals

Swim

Aerobic Endurance
Sets of 200s to 2000s at aerobic
pace, slower than threshold
Longer recovery

Muscular Endurance
Aerobic to threshold pace,
sets from 2000 to 3000
Shorter recovery

Threshold
Threshold main sets of 100s to 1000s
Short recovery

Speed
Shorter sets of 50s to 200s
Long recovery

Tri-Specific
Anaerobic to aerobic sets with fast
starts and longer threshold efforts
Range of recovery

Neuromuscular
Short, fast sets of 50 or less
working on turnover, not fitness
Long recovery

Bike

*(Note: Categories are based
on Dr. Andrew Coggan's zones.)*

Aerobic Recovery
Base-building and recovery
Heart rate zone 1
Power at <56% of FTP (zone 1)

Endurance
Aerobic, sometimes with long
anaerobic intervals

Heart rate and power zones 1 and 2
with brief spikes into zone 3
Power at 56–75% of FTP (zone 2)

Tempo
Steady state and longer intervals
Heart rate zones 2 and 3
Power at 76–90% of FTP (zones 2 and 3)
Short to moderate recovery
of 1:1 effort-to-recovery or less

Lactate Threshold
Interval work with hard efforts
ranging from 2–10 minutes
Heart rate zones 3 and 4
Power at 91–105% of FTP (zone 4)
Short to moderate recovery,
less than the time of the hard effort

VO$_2$max
Interval work with hard efforts
ranging from 1–6 minutes, few repeats
Heart rate zones 4 and 5a
Power at 106–120% of FTP
(high zone 4 to 5)
Moderate, active recovery

Anaerobic Capacity
Interval work with short, hard efforts
ranging from 15 seconds to 3 minutes
Heart rate zones 5a and 5b when
possible to get an accurate reading
(short duration can make it difficult)
Power at 121–150% of FTP (zone 6)
Limited recovery

Neuromuscular Power
Near max effort
Heart rate zones are difficult to read
due to short duration
Power at 150% of FTP
or greater (zone 7)
Moderate recovery

Force

Max force on the pedals, big gear; high effort, short intervals

Heart rate zones are difficult to read due to short duration

Power at 150% of FTP or greater (zone 7)

Big recovery

Power Development

Low cadence (40–60 rpm) efforts ranging from 1–15 minutes on hills or a big gear

Heart rate zone 3

Power at 76–90% of FTP (zone 3)

Moderate recovery

Run

Aerobic Recovery

Base-building and recovery

Heart rate, pace, and power zones 1 and 2

Tempo

Steady-state efforts and longer intervals of over 10 minutes

Heart rate and pace zones 3 and 4

Power at 89–104% of Run FTP

Moderate recovery

Speed Strength

Hill work and run with intervals from 10 seconds throughout entire session

Heart rate and pace zones 2 to 5a

Power at 89–124% of Run FTP (zones 3–6)

Moderate to no recovery

Speed Endurance

Longer intervals from 400–5000m

Heart rate and pace zones 3 to 5a

Power at 89–114% of Run FTP (zones 3–5)

Short recovery of 1:1 ratio of effort-to-recovery or less

VO$_2$max

High-intensity intervals from 30 seconds to 3 minutes

Heart rate and pace zones 4 to 5b

Active recovery in heart rate zones 2 to 3

Power at 105–114% of Run FTP (zone 5), recovery in zone 2

Anaerobic Speed

High-intensity speed intervals from 100–800m

Heart rate and pace zones from 4 to 5c

Power at 105–125+% of Run FTP (zones 5–7)

Limited recovery

Neuromuscular

Short, fast work near the end of an aerobic run, 200m or less

Heart rate, pace, and power zones spike to 5+

Full recovery

Long Run

Endurance runs with steady aerobic or specified pacing

Heart rate and pace zones from 1 to 5a

Power at 65–114% of Run FTP (zones 1–5)

Varied recovery

Strength Training

Anatomical Adaptation

Lighter weight, feeling easy, proper form learning the range of motion

Adapting the body to weight training

Fitness Strength

Weight should feel heavy, but not overwhelming; lift in control

Gaining strength while working on sport-specific fitness

Pure Strength 1

Heavier weights than the last phase, but workouts should fatigue the body less

Focus is on swim, bike, and run workouts while building strength

Pure Strength 2

Should be very heavy, but with perfect form

Short strength training workouts leave more room to feel fresh for swim, bike, or run

TABLE 6.2. The Big Picture

WEEKS ▶	1	2	3	4	5	6	7	8	9	10	11	12	13	14	15	16
	PHASE 1		PHASE 2						PHASE 3						PHASE 4	
	PREP 1	PREP 2	BASE 1	BASE 1	BASE 1	BASE 2	BASE 2	BASE 2	BUILD 1	BUILD 1	BUILD 1	BUILD 2	BUILD 2	BUILD 2	PEAK	RACE

Swim

	1	2	3	4	5	6	7	8	9	10	11	12	13	14	15	16
Aerobic endurance	■	■	■	■	■	■	■	■	■	■	■	■	■	■	■	
Muscular endurance						■	■	■	■	■	■	■	■	■	■	
Threshold			■	■	■	■	■	■	■	■	■	■	■	■	■	
Speed									■	■	■	■	■	■	■	
Tri-specific									■	■	■	■	■	■	■	

Bike

	1	2	3	4	5	6	7	8	9	10	11	12	13	14	15	16
Aerobic recovery	■	■				■			■	■	■	■	■	■	■	
Endurance	■	■	■	■	■	■	■	■	■	■	■	■	■	■	■	
Tempo	■	■	■	■	■	■	■	■	■	■	■	■	■	■	■	
Lactate threshold									■	■	■	■	■	■	■	
VO$_2$max									■	■	■	■	■	■	■	
Anaerobic capacity									■	■	■	■	■	■	■	
Neuromuscular power	■	■	■	■	■	■	■	■	■	■	■	■	■	■	■	
Power development			■	■	■	■	■	■	■	■	■	■	■	■		

Run

	1	2	3	4	5	6	7	8	9	10	11	12	13	14	15	16
Aerobic recovery	■	■	■	■	■	■	■	■	■	■	■	■	■	■	■	
Tempo						■	■	■	■	■	■	■	■	■	■	
Speed strength						■	■	■	■	■	■	■	■	■		
Speed endurance						■	■	■	■	■	■	■	■	■	■	
VO$_2$max									■	■	■	■	■	■	■	
Anaerobic speed									■	■	■	■	■	■	■	
Neuromuscular	■	■	■	■	■	■	■	■	■	■	■	■	■	■	■	
Long run	■	■	■	■	■	■	■	■	■	■	■	■	■	■	■	

Strength

	1	2	3	4	5	6	7	8	9	10	11	12	13	14	15	16
Anatomical adapt.	■	■														
Fitness strength			■	■	■	■	■	■								
Pure strength 1									■	■	■					
Pure strength 2												■	■			

MISSED DAYS

Plans provide a structured pathway to get from the first day of training to the starting line, but let's be realistic: Sometimes things come up, lives get hectic, and plans change. Even the best intentions can get sidetracked when the unexpected crops up. The good news about short-course triathlon is that it plays well with life! Here we'll address some of the situations that may arise in the 16 weeks before your race. We'll look at how to cope with unscheduled curveballs and what to do when they happen.

ONE DAY MISSED: If you miss a day because of . . . well, anything . . . you can simply skip that day's training and move on to the next day. Do not try to make up the workout by cramming it into the next day's training schedule or by pushing everything else back. Each workout has a specific amount of recovery time post-session. If you try to stack them up, you'll be missing the only thing more important than hitting that mileage: recovery. You'll run right into the next workout, you'll become even more fatigued (even if that following workout is light), and you could launch a spiral of energy depletion. One day that's a little off is no big deal, but if you get into a recovery deficit, oftentimes you won't feel the effects until a week later, and you'll need to take quite a bit of time off to recover. The same thing goes for hitting weekly hour totals—those are only to be used as a planning guide, not as a target to be hit at all costs. If you miss a day, basically scratch out that week's total, pretend it never existed, and you'll be fine.

TWO TO THREE DAYS MISSED: The strategy here is similar to missing a single day, with caveats. First, if you find yourself missing more than a day, it's likely due to outside stressors such as sickness, travel, work, or obligations. Trying to make up for missed workouts (or stretching yourself thin to hit them all on their prescribed days) will only add to that stress. Remind yourself that you won't have lost any significant amount of fitness in a few days that can't be regained over consistent training in the coming weeks. Again, an advantage of short-course racing is that you're not going from a heavy training load to none—the gap is not as great as with long-course training.

Second, *how* you come back from a few missed days depends on why you missed those days in the first place. Generally speaking, if your first day back from a break is a high-intensity workout, substitute something easier. After time off, too much volume or intensity can be a shock to the system and cause the potential for injury. Just as when getting into a hot shower, you don't want to jump in too fast. But if you missed those days due to illness or injury, it's important to keep the workload light for the first *three* days back. The rule of thumb is that the first day back should be at 60 percent of the planned intensity, the second day back should be at 75 percent, and day *three* should be at 90 percent. The goal is to slowly dial up the "heat."

A WEEK OR MORE MISSED: Don't panic. Research shows that even after a full week off, athletes lose only a negligible amount of fitness; even after two weeks of missed workouts, athletes only lose about 5 percent of their fitness. But you still need to readjust the plan in order to build back into the program safely. The best way to come back—the only way, really—is through patient consistency. Pick up where you should be now, not where you were before the break. Avoid intensity for the first five days. Adjust the schedule, keeping the prescribed sports the same, but no intensity at zone 4 and above. Keep it aerobic. Build up volume gradually—day 1: 50 percent, day 2: 65 percent, day 3: 75 percent, day 4: 90 percent, day 5: 100 percent, all still under zone 4. By day 6, you should be ready to get back to full speed.

Use this speed bump in your plan to analyze what you think went wrong. Obviously some things are unavoidable, but in order to avoid sickness or injury, recommit to eating healthy, taking care of your body, and getting proper rest. If your health was compromised for some reason, it may need a little more care than you had thought.

> In short course, you really want to try to race right under your redline for the entire race—just under that point where you are going to absolutely explode.
>
> —2009 ITU Long-Course World Champion Tim O'Donnell

MISSING MORE THAN TWO WEEKS: It's time to adjust your goals. Consider looking at a different race date and restarting training from week 1 with your eyes on a new goal 16 weeks out. If that's not possible, restart your training with the pattern above, keeping in mind that you'll have plenty of room for improvement on your next event.

When Time Is Limited

It's important to carve out the proper amount of time to do the workouts, but sometimes things get in the way. Let's say your workout calls for an hour of running, but you only have a half-hour to give in your day. What should you do? Go ahead and cut the workout short, reminding yourself that doing something is always better than doing nothing. When cutting a workout short, there are a few rules to bear in mind.

For aerobic workouts, simply amend the volume (time or distance) to fit the time you have, while keeping the intensity the same. Don't increase the intensity because your workout has gone from an hour to 30 minutes. Go the same pace you were supposed to for an hour, but just do half as much time.

For interval workouts, there is an "order of priority" for what to carve off the "meat" of the workout:

1. **ELIMINATE THE COOLDOWN.** Though a good strategy for returning your body back to a rest state, physiologically, the cooldown is the least important phase in a hard interval workout.

2. **CUT THE WARM-UP BY 50 PERCENT.** The warm-up is far more important than the cooldown, but you'll still be able to perform adequately—if not at your absolute best—with a reduced warm-up. Also, the risk for injury is still greatly reduced with a 50 percent warm-up.

3. **ELIMINATE INTERVALS.** If you're still not able to complete a given interval workout, even with the above cuts, start cutting repeats. Cut as much as you need to get the workout in, but not more than 50 percent—at that point, it might be worth writing off the session altogether, using it as a recovery day, and picking up the plan the next day. Unlike when amending the aerobic workout, it's okay to increase the intensity during the intervals, given you'll be doing less, but remember to remain in control.

Upping Your Volume

We caution against adding more volume. The best thing about following a plan is that it does not focus on a day or two, rather it's crafted with the long-term and your overall progression in mind. If you opt to overdo it with extra mileage, the effect may compromise workouts in the days that follow. Fatigue may not manifest until weeks later, and by then it will be difficult to dig out of the overtraining hole you've created. Follow the plan.

THE LEVEL 1 PROGRAM

New challenges are both exciting and intimidating. It might feel like there's a lot to figure out when you're juggling three sports consecutively—and there is, at first—but once you've mastered the basics, triathlon is actually pretty simple. By this point in the book, you've learned about history, gear, technique, supplementary work, and strategy. This chapter presents you with a trusted map to follow on the next part of your tri journey: the Level 1 Program. In 16 weeks, the Level 1 Program is designed to take you from inexperienced endurance athlete to the starting line of a short-course triathlon. So buckle up and get ready for an exciting, life-changing, and possibly quite tiring experience. Our hope is that you'll emerge on the other side of race day feeling more confident and motivated to continue your tri adventure, either by repeating this plan and refining your race or transitioning up the next levels of triathlon training with the Level 2 and 3 Programs contained in this book.

There's a lot to learn, but we'll take it one step at a time. Start by familiarizing yourself with the terms that follow, then review the plan, pick a race, and dive into day one!

GAUGE YOUR EFFORT

We've included Rate of Perceived Exertion (RPE) and heart-rate zones in the pages that follow to help measure your intensity during certain workouts. RPE is by far the most low-tech and basic way to judge your effort, as it goes by how you feel. Despite its simplicity, it's still an important way to train and race. If you'd like to take your training a step further, you can use a heart-rate monitor to work out according to your heart-rate zones. If you choose to go with RPE, you can treat the zone tests scattered throughout the Level 1 plan as benchmarks to help track your progress instead. If you use heart rate, be sure to complete the tests, as your zones will change as you improve.

THE LINGO

Triathlon has its own language. Words such as "brick," "body marking" and "T1 and T2" might sound made up, but they actually help communicate important concepts. Here we've collected some of the lingo that you'll need to know while using this book and out on the course:

AID STATION: A predetermined area on the course where athletes can pick up food or drinks. Every race's aid station offerings vary greatly, so be sure to check the race information prior in order to know what they'll be "serving."

ATHENA/CLYDESDALE DIVISION: Rather than breaking down the results into age groups, some eligible racers may opt into this weight-based category. For USAT, the men's cutoff is 220 pounds and above; the women's is 165 pounds and above.

BODY MARKING: Before race start on race morning, many events require volunteers to write each competitor's number and age group or category on the racer's body. Some events offer temporary tattoos that must be applied prior to the start instead.

BRICK: A workout that combines two or more sports. For instance, a swim-bike brick would involve both swimming and biking in one session—sometimes with a break in between, sometimes in different orders, sometimes as a race-day simulation you'll find built into the plan.

CADENCE: Usually written in strokes for how many times your hands enter the water in a given interval, revolutions per minute (rpm) for how quickly your legs spin in cycling, and strides per minute (spm) for how often your feet touch the ground.

DRAFTING: This term is usually referring to "sitting" behind another competitor while on the bike leg and is illegal in the vast majority of races, except for explicit "draft-legal" events. USAT rules say athletes must stay three bike lengths behind the rider in front of them. Drafting can also refer to sitting behind another athlete in the swim or run, and this is *not* illegal, but rather an excellent skill that gives a tangible (and fair) advantage.

OPEN-WATER SWIMMING: Training or racing in a body of water—not a pool—where there are no lane lines or walls to hang on to.

PENALTY: A penalty is assessed by an on-course race marshal. Sometimes the penalty requires the athlete to stop racing for a set amount of time indicated by the race marshal; sometimes the penalty is simply added to the racer's final overall time. For specifics on penalties, be sure to check in with your race's governing body or race director.

> Short-course racing is intense and fun at the same time. One of the blessings of short-course racing is that if it isn't your day, you don't have to suffer too long.
>
> —2004 Olympian Andy Potts

PR: Shorthand for "personal record," an acronym used to indicate a person's fastest time for the course or distance.

RACE PACKET: Essential information distributed by the race organizers that must be picked up prior to racing. This usually includes your race number and detailed race-day instructions.

SPLIT: In workouts, this is a segment of time within the overall workout. In racing, this can indicate a "negative split" (going faster at the end of your race than at the beginning), a "positive split" (slowing down as the race goes on), or be used to describe the time spent while swimming, biking, or running.

START WAVE: Most short-course events don't have a mass start where all triathletes begin at the same time, so instead, groups broken down by gender, age, or skill level start together. Finish times are recorded from the start of each person's wave and put into an aggregate list for overall standings.

T1 AND T2: Terms used to describe the transition from swimming to biking and biking to running, respectively.

TIMING CHIP: A chip is often used to time your race. Usually included in the race packet or picked up pre-race, the chip is generally attached to a Velcro strap and worn around the ankle.

TRAINER: A piece of equipment that allows an everyday bicycle to be ridden stationary indoors.

TRANSITION: The time between legs of a triathlon. There is usually a specific transition area where triathletes keep gear to use for each sport. Time spent in the transition area is recorded separately on results and then added to your overall time.

	SESSION 1	SESSION 2
Mon.	**REST DAY**	
Tues.	**RUN** **Aerobic Base Building // 30 min.** 30 min. RPE <4, Z1/Z2 *Light and easy with good form.* *Cadence at 90+ spm.*	**SWIM** **Aerobic Endurance Form Work // 1900** **Warm-up:** 100 swim, 100 kick, 100 pull, all with 30 sec. rest **Main set:** 6 × 100 easy, 30 sec. rest 4 × 200 easy, 30 sec. rest **Cooldown:** 4 × 50, 20 sec. rest *Focus on form. Aim for 55–70 strokes/min.*
Wed.	**BIKE** **Endurance Base Building // 50 min.** 50 min. RPE <4, Z1/Z2 *Keep cadence high.*	
Thurs.	**SWIM** **Aerobic Endurance Intervals // 1450** **Warm-up:** 100 easy swim, 50 easy kick, 100 moderate swim, 50 moderate kick, 100 swim build speed, 50 kick build speed, all with 15 sec. rest **Main set:** 2 × 300 moderate, 10 sec. rest Rest 2 min. between sets 100 kick, steady 4 × 50 relaxed speed, 15 sec. rest **Cooldown:** 100 easy *Decrease times with each work interval for the first set.*	**STRENGTH** **Anatomical Adaptation // 1 hr.** *See p. 252 for exercises.*

SESSION 1	SESSION 2
Fri.	
RUN **Aerobic Recovery** // 20 min. 20 min. RPE 1–2, Z1 *Controlled and relaxed.*	**BIKE** **Aerobic Recovery** // 30 min. 30 min. RPE 1–2, Z1 *Focus on smooth, even pedal stroke.*
Sat.	
SWIM **Aerobic Endurance Drills** // 1400 **Warm-up:** 400 choice **Main set:** 8 × 50 drills for technique limiter, 20 sec. rest 6 × 50 fast with good form, 30 sec. rest **Cooldown:** 300 easy	**RUN** **Aerobic Moderate Mid-Distance** // **40 min.** 40 min. RPE <6, Z1–Z3 *Mostly RPE <4, Z1/Z2. Flat to rolling terrain.* *Aerobic work with good form.*
Sun.	
BIKE **Endurance Pure Base** // 1 hr. 60 min. RPE <6, Z1–Z3 *It's okay to spike the power a bit into RPE 6, Z3 on* *hills or into headwinds. Mostly smooth and steady,* *pure base building.*	

**HERE WE GO! THIS PHASE IS DESIGNED TO GET YOU UP
AND RUNNING. FIRST, A BUILD WEEK, THEN NEXT WEEK IS
YOUR FIRST ROUND OF BASELINE TESTS.**

TOTAL » 7 HR. 10 MIN.

	SESSION 1	SESSION 2
Mon.	**REST DAY**	
Tues.	**RUN** **LTHR Test // 50 min.** *If you do not have a heart rate monitor, treat this as a benchmark test. See pp. 235–236 for details.*	**SWIM** **Aerobic Endurance // 1800** **Warm-up:** 200 swim, 100 kick, 200 pull, all with 30 sec. rest 4 × 50 drill, 15 sec. rest **Main set:** Rest 1 min. between sets: 4 × 150 easier than threshold, 10 sec. rest 4 × 75 easier than threshold, 10 sec. rest 4 × 25 fast, 30 sec. rest **Cooldown:** 100 choice
Wed.	**BIKE** **LTHR Test // 50 min.** *If you do not have a heart rate monitor, treat this as a benchmark test. See pp. 235–236 for details.*	
Thurs.	**SWIM** **STP Test // 2100** *See p. 234 for details.*	**STRENGTH** **Anatomical Adaptation // 1 hr.** *See p. 252 for exercises.*

LEVEL 1

	SESSION 1	SESSION 2
Fri.	**RUN**	**BIKE**
	Aerobic Recovery // 20 min.	**Aerobic Recovery // 30 min.**
	20 min. RPE 1–2, Z1	30 min. easy spin RPE 1–2, Z1
	Controlled and relaxed.	*Focus on a smooth, even pedal stroke.*
Sat.	**RUN**	**SWIM**
	Aerobic Moderate Mid-Distance // 55 min.	**Aerobic Endurance Form Work // 1900**
	55 min. RPE <6, Z1–Z3	**Warm-up:** 100 swim, 100 kick, 100 pull, all with 30 sec. rest
	Mostly RPE <4, Z1/Z2. Flat to rolling terrain. Aerobic work with good form.	**Main set:** Easy effort: 6 × 100, 30 sec. rest 4 × 200, 30 sec. rest
		Cooldown: 200 easy
		Focus on form. Aim for 55–70 strokes/min.
Sun.	**BIKE**	
	Endurance Pure Base // 1 hr. 30 min.	
	90 min. RPE <6, Z1–Z3	
	It's okay to spike the power a bit into RPE 6, Z3 on hills or into headwinds. Mostly smooth and steady, pure base building.	

TOTAL » 8 HR. 50 MIN.

LEVEL 1

	SESSION 1	SESSION 2
Mon.	**REST DAY**	

Tues.	**SWIM**
	
	Aerobic Endurance // **2400**
	
	Warm-up: 200 swim, 100 kick, 200 pull, all with 30 sec. rest
	4 × 50 drill, 15 sec. rest
	Main set:
	2 sets:
	    3 × 200 at threshold + 10 sec., 15 sec. rest
	    200 pull, 2 min. rest
	Cooldown: 100 choice
		RUN
		
		Neuromuscular // **40 min.**
		
		Warm-up: 30 min. RPE <4, Z1/Z2
		Main set:
		6 × 30 strides RPE 6, with walking recoveries
		Cooldown: 5 min.
		
		Strides are best done on grass or soft surface. Aim for 19–20 sec. Fast but controlled.

Wed.	**BRICK** **Bike Endurance Progression + Aerobic Run** // **1 hr. 25 min.** **Main set:** 70 min. ride **Run off the bike:** 15 min. RPE <4, Z1/Z2 *First part of ride should be in RPE <4, Z1/Z2. Average in RPE 3–6, Z2/Z3 at halfway point; avoid RPE 7, Z4. For the run, just find your legs and hold steady.*	
Thurs.	**SWIM** **Muscular Endurance** // **2400** **Warm-up:** 200 choice, 30 sec. rest 5 × 100 descend 1–5 (each set faster than previous), 30 sec. rest **Main set:** 500 steady, 30 sec. rest 400 as 75 easy/25 fast, 1 min. rest 6 × 100 race pace, 15 sec. rest **Cooldown:** 200 easy	**STRENGTH** **Fitness Strength** // **1 hr.** *See p. 252 for exercises.*

	SESSION 1	SESSION 2
Fri.	**RUN** **Aerobic Recovery** // **20 min.** 20 min. RPE 2, Z1 *Controlled and relaxed.*	**BIKE** **Endurance Base Building** // **40 min.** 40 min. RPE <4, Z1/Z2 *Keep cadence high.*
Sat.	**RUN** **Aerobic Rolling Course** // **1 hr.** 60 min. RPE <6, Z1–Z3 *Focus on proud, upright form. Allow heart rate to gradually rise to Z3, but don't force it up.*	**SWIM** **Aerobic Endurance Drills** // **1400** **Warm-up:** 400 choice of free, stroke, pull, and kick **Main set:** 8 × 50 drills for technique limiter, 20 sec. rest 6 × 50 fast with good form, 30 sec. rest **Cooldown:** 300 easy
Sun.	**BIKE** **Endurance Cadence Drills** // **1 hr. 30 min.** **Warm-up:** 30 min. **Main set:** 6 × 1 min. on, RPE <7, Z3/Z4/ 1 min. off 10 min. spin 2 × 5 min. on, RPE 6, Z3/ 5 min. off 2 × 1 min. on, RPE <7, Z3/Z4/ 1 min. off **Cooldown:** 14 min. *Increase cadence to 100 rpm for 5 min. "on" intervals. Easy spin for "off" intervals.*	

STARTING TO BUILD SOME GOOD BASE!

TOTAL » 9 HR. 40 MIN.

LEVEL 1

	SESSION 1	SESSION 2
Mon.	**REST DAY**	

Tues.

RUN

Neuromuscular // 50 min.

Warm-up: 35 min. RPE <6, Z1–Z3
Main set:
6 × 200m strides RPE 6, with 200m jog recoveries
Cooldown: 5 min.

Build from slow to fast with each stride set.

SWIM

Aerobic Endurance // 2600

Warm-up: 200 swim, 200 kick, 200 pull, all with 30 sec. rest
6 × 50 drill or stroke (no free), 15 sec. rest
Main set:
3 sets:
   400 free at 100 threshold pace + 5 sec., 20 sec. rest
   100 kick, 30 sec. rest
Cooldown: 200 easy

Wed.

BRICK

Tempo Bike + Aerobic Run // 1 hr. 35 min.

Warm-up: 20 min. ride
Main set:
45 min. RPE 5–6, Z3
Cooldown: 15 min. spin
Run off the bike: 15 min. RPE <4, Z1/Z2

For the run, just find your legs and hold steady.

Thurs.

SWIM

Muscular Endurance // 2800

Warm-up: 200 swim, 100 kick, 200 pull, all with 30 sec. rest
6 × 50 drill, 15 sec. rest
Main set:
   100 threshold pace + 5 sec.
   500 free, 400 pull, each with 20 sec. rest
   300 free, 200 kick or stroke (no free), each with 15 sec. rest
100 free fast, 1 min. rest
3 × 100 at threshold, 10 sec. rest
Cooldown: 200 swim

STRENGTH

Fitness Strength // 1 hr.

See p. 252 for exercises.

	SESSION 1	SESSION 2
Fri.	**RUN**	**BIKE**
	Aerobic Base Building // **30 min.**	**Endurance Base Building** // **45 min.**
	30 min. RPE <4, Z1/Z2	45 min. RPE <4, Z1/Z2
	Light and easy with good form. *Cadence at 90+ spm.*	*Keep cadence high.*
Sat.	**RUN**	**SWIM**
	Aerobic Rolling Course // **1 hr. 15 min.**	**Aerobic Endurance Drills** // **1400**
	75 min. RPE <6, Z1–Z3	**Warm-up:** 400 choice
	Focus on proud, upright form. Allow heart rate to gradually rise to Z3, but don't force it up.	**Main set:** 8 × 50 drills for technique limiter, 20 sec. rest 6 × 50 fast with good form, 30 sec. rest **Cooldown:** 300 easy
Sun.	**BRICK**	
	Endurance Bike + Aerobic Run // **1 hr. 45 min.**	
	Warm-up: 15 min. ride **Main set:** 60 min. RPE <6, Z2/Z3 with 8 sec. out-of-saddle bursts every 10 min., RPE 8 **Cooldown:** 15 min. spin **Run off the bike:** 15 min. RPE <4, Z1/Z2	
	Relatively high cadence for the bike warm-up, 90 rpm. Bursts should be 80% of a full sprint, 105+ rpm. For the run, just find your legs and hold steady.	

TOTAL » 10 HR. 5 MIN.

	SESSION 1	SESSION 2
Mon.	**REST DAY**	
Tues.	**SWIM** **Aerobic Endurance // 1600** **Warm-up:** 200 swim, 100 kick, 200 pull, all with 30 sec. rest 4 × 50 drill, 15 sec. rest **Main set:** 300 swim at threshold + 5 sec., 15 sec. rest 200 steady swim at threshold + 5 sec., 15 sec. rest 100 fast, 1 min. rest 100 kick **Cooldown:** 200 swim	**RUN** **Aerobic Moderate Mid-Distance // 40 min.** 40 min. RPE <6, Z1–Z3 *Mostly RPE <4, Z1/Z2. Flat to rolling terrain. Aerobic work with good form.*
Wed.	**BIKE** **Neuromuscular Power // 1 hr.** **Warm-up:** 30 min. RPE <4, Z1/Z2 **Main set:** 8 spin-ups RPE 8, 2 min. recovery RPE 2, Z1 **Cooldown:** 10 min. *When you start to bounce in the saddle, back off and recover. Don't push a big gear. Keep your legs sharp and increase cadence, not power.*	
Thurs.	**SWIM** **Muscular Endurance // 2100** **Warm-up:** 200 swim, 100 kick, 200 pull, all with 30 sec. rest 4 × 50 drill, 15 sec. rest **Main set:** 4 × 250 as 100 moderate/50 fast/100 moderate, 20 sec. rest 1 min. rest 300 with second 150 10 sec. faster than first, 30 sec. rest 1 min. rest **Cooldown:** 100 swim	**STRENGTH** **Fitness Strength // 1 hr.** *See p. 252 for exercises.*

	SESSION 1	SESSION 2
Fri.	**RUN** **Aerobic Recovery // 20 min.** 20 min. RPE 2, Z1 *Controlled and relaxed.*	**BIKE** **Aerobic Recovery // 30 min.** 30 min. RPE 2, Z1 *Focus on smooth, even pedal stroke.*
Sat.	**RUN** **Aerobic Long Run // 1 hr.** 1 hr. *Get at least half of the time in RPE 3–4, Z2. Focus on good form and quick cadence.*	**SWIM** **Aerobic Endurance Form Work // 2200** **Warm-up:** 300 choice 6 × 50 drill, 15 sec. rest. **Main set:** Easy effort 6 × 100, 30 sec. rest 4 × 200, 30 sec. rest **Cooldown:** 100 kick, 100 swim *Focus on form. Aim for 55–70 strokes/min.*
Sun.	**BIKE** **Endurance Recovery // 1 hr. 10 min.** 70 min. RPE <4, Z1/Z2 *Don't exceed RPE 4, Z2 for more than a few seconds at a time as when accelerating from a stop or going up a short hill. Comfortably high rpm.*	

LIGHTER THIS WEEK. LET THE BODY AND MIND RECOVER
FROM THE LAST TWO WEEKS OF SOLID BASE BUILDING.

TOTAL » 9 HR. 10 MIN.

LEVEL 1

	SESSION 1	SESSION 2
Mon.	**REST DAY**	
Tues.	**RUN** **Tempo // 1 hr.** **Warm-up:** 20 min. RPE <4, Z1/Z2 **Main set:** 20 min. RPE <6, Z2/Z3 20 min. steady RPE 5–6, Z3 *Pace and heart rate should progressively increase as the run progresses.*	**SWIM** **Muscular Endurance // 2400** **Warm-up:** 400 choice; 6 × 50 drill, 15 sec. rest **Main set:** 300 swim, 300 pull, each with 15 sec. rest 100 fast swim, 1 min. rest 200 swim, 200 pull, each with 15 sec. rest 100 fast swim, 1 min. rest 100 swim, 100 pull, each with 15 sec. rest 100 fast swim, 1 min. rest **Cooldown:** 200 choice
Wed.	**BRICK** **Bike Power Development + Aerobic Run // 1 hr. 30 min.** **Warm-up:** 20 min. on bike, RPE <4, Z1/Z2 **Main set:** 3 min. at 40 rpm, 2 min. recovery 6 min. at 50 rpm, 3 min. recovery 12 min. at 60 rpm, 4 min. recovery 6 min. at 50 rpm, 3 min. recovery 3 min. at 40 rpm, 2 min. recovery **Cooldown:** 11 min. very easy spin **Run off the bike:** 15 min. RPE <4, Z1/Z2 *Bike recoveries should all be in RPE 1–2, Z1 at a cadence of 80–100 rpm. Intervals should go from RPE 7, low Z4 in the shortest sets to RPE 5–6, Z3 in the longest. For the run, just find your legs and hold steady.*	
Thurs.	**SWIM** **Threshold // 3100** **Warm-up:** 400 choice 4 × 50 drill, 15 sec. rest **Main set:** Rest 1 min. between sets: 3 × 350 swim/pull/swim at threshold, 20 sec. rest 3 × 250 swim/pull/swim at threshold, 20 sec. rest 3 × 150 swim/pull/swim at threshold, 20 sec. rest 3 × 50 swim/pull/swim at threshold, 20 sec. rest **Cooldown:** 100 swim	**STRENGTH** **Fitness Strength // 1 hr.** *See p. 252 for exercises.*

	SESSION 1	SESSION 2
Fri.	**RUN** **Neuromuscular** // **30 min.** **Warm-up:** 20 min. RPE <4, Z1/Z2 **Main set:** 6 × 30 strides RPE 6, with walking recoveries **Cooldown:** 5 min. *Strides are best done on grass or soft surface. Aim for 19–20 sec. Fast but controlled.*	**BIKE** **Endurance Base Building** // **45 min.** 45 min. RPE <4, Z1/Z2 *Keep cadence high.*
Sat.	**RUN** **Long Run** // **1 hr. 15 min.** 75 min. *The first 45 min. of the run are all aerobic RPE <4, in Z1 and Z2. Tempo finish in last 30 min., RPE 5–6, Z3. Relax! Record your tempo pace during the last 30 min.*	**SWIM** **Aerobic Endurance Drills** // **1400** **Warm-up:** 400 choice **Main set:** 8 × 50 drills for technique limiter, 20 sec. rest 6 × 50 fast with good form, 30 sec. rest **Cooldown:** 300 easy
Sun.	**BRICK** **Bike Endurance Intervals + Aerobic Run** // **2 hr. 25 min.** **Warm-up:** 30 min. ride **Main set:** 5 × 1 min. primer repeats, 2 min. recovery 4 × 15 min. repeats, 5 min. recovery **Cooldown:** 5 min. spin **Run off the bike:** 15 min. RPE <4, Z1/Z2 *Primer repeats in RPE 5–7, Z3/Z4. 15 min. repeats in RPE 5–6, Z3. This should feel smooth and steady. Lock in the pace and hold on. For the run, just find your legs and hold steady.*	

GETTING IN SOME MORE BASE WORK. VOLUME WILL CONTINUE TO INCREASE, AND INTENSITY WILL RISE JUST A BIT TOO.

TOTAL » 11 HR. 50 MIN.

LEVEL 1

	SESSION 1	SESSION 2
Mon.	**REST DAY**	
Tues.	**RUN** **Speed Strength // 1 hr. 5 min.** **Warm-up:** 30 min. moderate run **Main set:** 10 × 80m hill sprints, RPE 7–8, Z4 Jog downhill for recovery 2 miles at tempo, RPE <7, Z3–Z4 **Cooldown:** 5 min. jog *Do the hill sprints on a 6–10% grade.* *Fast and powerful.*	**SWIM** **Muscular Endurance // 2500** **Warm-up:** 200 swim, 100 kick, 200 pull, all with 30 sec. rest 6 × 50 drill or stroke (no free), 10 sec. rest **Main set:** 2 × 300 steady pull, 15 sec. rest 4 × 150 threshold swim, 10 sec. rest 6 × 50 speed swim, 30 sec. rest 100 easy kick **Cooldown:** 100 easy
Wed.	**BRICK** **Bike Power Development + Aerobic Run // 1 hr. 40 min.** **Warm-up:** 15 min. on the bike **Main set:** 6 × 5 min. at 55 rpm, 5 min. recovery **Cooldown:** 10 min. spin **Run off the bike:** 15 min. RPE <4, Z1/Z2 *Do 5 min. intervals on flat or slightly uphill terrain in RPE 7, Z4. Constant pressure on the pedals.* *For the run, just find your legs and hold steady.*	

Thurs.	**SWIM**
	
	 Threshold // 2800
	
	 Warm-up: 200 swim, 100 kick, 200 pull, all with 30 sec. rest
	 4 × 50 drill or stroke (no free), 15 sec. rest
	 Main set:
	 2 sets:
	    300 steady pull, 20 sec. rest
	    5 × 100 at threshold, 10 sec. rest
	 1 min. rest
	 300 pull
	 Cooldown: 200 easy
		STRENGTH
		
		 Fitness Strength // 1 hr.
		
		 See p. 252 for exercises.

	SESSION 1	SESSION 2
Fri.	**RUN** **Neuromuscular // 30 min.** **Warm-up:** 20 min. RPE <4, Z1/Z2 **Main set:** 6 × 30 strides RPE 6, with walking recoveries **Cooldown:** 5 min. *Strides are best done on grass or soft surface.* *Aim for 19–20 sec. Fast but controlled.*	**BIKE** **Endurance Base Building // 45 min.** 45 min. RPE <4, Z1/Z2 *Keep cadence high.*
Sat.	**RUN** **Long Run // 1 hr. 20 min.** **Warm-up:** 20 min. **Main set:** 50 min. RPE <6, Z3 **Cooldown:** 10 min. *Focus on good form with cadence at 90+ rpm.*	**SWIM** **Aerobic Endurance Drills // 1400** **Warm-up:** 400 choice **Main set:** 8 × 50 drills for technique limiter, 20 sec. rest 6 × 50 fast with good form, 30 sec. rest **Cooldown:** 300 easy
Sun.	**BRICK** **Endurance Bike + Aerobic Run // 3 hr.** **Main set:** 2 hr. 45 min. ride **Run off the bike:** 15 min. *Ride should mostly be in RPE <4, Z1/Z2. Okay for* *effort to spike into RPE 6, Z3 every once in a while.* *Plan accordingly with nutrition and hydration.*	

TOTAL » 12 HR. 40 MIN.

	SESSION 1	SESSION 2
Mon.	**REST DAY**	
Tues.	**RUN** **LTHR Test** // **50 min.** *If you do not have a heart rate monitor, treat this as a benchmark test. See pp. 235–236 for details.*	**SWIM** **Muscular Endurance** // **2100** **Warm-up:** 100 swim, 100 kick, 100 pull, all with 30 sec. rest; 4 × 50 drill, 15 sec. rest **Main set:** 300 swim, 300 pull, each with 15 sec. rest 100 fast swim, 1 min. rest 200 swim, 200 pull, each with 15 sec. rest 100 fast swim, 1 min. rest 100 swim, 100 pull, each with 15 sec. rest 100 fast swim **Cooldown:** 100 choice
Wed.	**BIKE** **LTHR Test** // **50 min.** *If you do not have a heart rate monitor, treat this as a benchmark test. See pp. 235–236 for details.*	
Thurs.	**SWIM** **STP Test** // **2100** *See p. 234 for details.*	**STRENGTH** **Fitness Strength** // **1 hr.** *See p. 252 for exercises.*

	SESSION 1	SESSION 2
Fri.	**RUN** **Aerobic Recovery** // **15 min.** 15 min. RPE 1–2, Z1 *Controlled and relaxed.*	**BIKE** **Aerobic Recovery** // **30 min.** 30 min. RPE 1–2, Z1 *Focus on smooth, even pedal stroke.*
Sat.	**RUN** **Aerobic Long Run** // **50 min.** 50 min. *Get at least half of the time in RPE 3–4, Z2. Focus on good form and quick cadence.*	**SWIM** **Aerobic Endurance Form Work** // **1300** **Warm-up:** 200 choice **Main set:** Easy effort: 6 × 100, 30 sec. rest 2 × 200, 30 sec. rest **Cooldown:** 100 easy *Focus on form. Aim for 55–70 strokes/min.*
Sun.	**BIKE** **Endurance Recovery** // **1 hr. 15 min.** 75 min. RPE <4, Z1/Z2 *Don't exceed RPE 4, Z2 for more than a few seconds at a time as when accelerating from a stop or going up a short hill. Keep cadence comfortably high.*	

BACKING OFF THE TRAINING A BIT AND GETTING IN SOME
CHECK–IN TESTS. AFTER EACH TEST, YOU'LL NEED TO MODIFY
YOUR TRAINING ZONES IF YOU ARE USING A HEART RATE MONITOR.

TOTAL » 8 HR. 20 MIN.

	SESSION 1	SESSION 2
Mon.	**REST DAY**	
Tues.	**SWIM** **Muscular Endurance // 2400** **Warm-up:** 200 swim, 100 kick, 200 pull, all with 30 sec. rest 4 × 50 drill, 15 sec. rest **Main set:** 100 kick, 200 swim, each with 15 sec. rest 300 pull, 400 swim, 300 pull, all with 20 sec. rest 200 swim, 15 sec. rest 100 kick, 1 min. rest **Cooldown:** 100 easy	**RUN** **Speed Strength // 55 min.** **Warm-up:** 15 min. **Main set:** 4 × 800m uphill run Jog downhill to recover **Cooldown:** 10 min. easy *Hill should be 4–6% grade. Build to RPE 7, Z4 on each set. Focus on driving the legs and arms up the hill.*

Wed.	**BRICK**
	Bike Neuromuscular Power + Aerobic Run // 1 hr. 25 min.
	Warm-up: 15 min. ride
	Main set:
	3 sets:
	  10 min. as 15 sec. on, RPE 9/
	  15 sec. off, RPE 2, Z1
	Spin 5 min. between sets RPE <4
	Cooldown: 10 min. ride
	Run off the bike: 15 min. RPE <4, Z1/Z2
	For the run, just find your legs and hold steady.	

Thurs.	**SWIM**
	Tri-Specific // 2900
	Warm-up: 200 swim, 100 kick, 200 swim, all with 30 sec. rest
	6 × 50 drill or stroke (no free), 15 sec. rest
	Main set:
	2 sets:
	  200 fast, 10 sec. rest
	  300 steady swim, 15 sec. rest
	  400 pull, 30 sec. rest
	8 × 25 fast, 30 sec. rest
	Cooldown: 100 easy
		STRENGTH
		Pure Strength 1 // 45 min.
		See p. 252 for exercises.

LEVEL 1

SESSION 1	SESSION 2
Fri.	

RUN

Neuromuscular // 30 min.

Warm-up: 20 min. RPE <4, Z1/Z2
Main set:
6 × 30 strides RPE 6, with walking recoveries
Cooldown: 5 min.

Strides are best done on grass or soft surface. Aim for 19–20 sec. Fast but controlled.

BIKE

Endurance Isolated-Leg Training // 45 min.

Warm-up: 20 min.
Main set:
20 min. as 1 min. left/1 min. right RPE 5
Get a total of 10 min. on each leg
Cooldown: 5 min. spin

Do this on a trainer to have non-pedaling leg on a chair. Keep comfortably high cadence. Focus on eliminating dead spot in stroke by pushing toes forward in shoes at top.

Sat.

RUN

Long Run // 1 hr. 20 min.

Warm-up: 20 min.
Main set:
5 sets:
  1200m RPE 7, Z4
  400m jog recovery
Cooldown: Easy jog for duration

This should be high quality. Focus on good efforts during the 1200s.

SWIM

Aerobic Endurance Drills // 1300

Warm-up: 400 choice
Main set:
8 × 50 drills for technique limiter, 20 sec. rest
6 × 50 fast with good form, 30 sec. rest
Cooldown: 200 easy

Sun.

BRICK

Tempo Bike + Tempo Run // 2 hr. 30 min.

Warm-up: 40 min. ride
Main set:
45 min. tempo RPE 5–7, Z3/Z4
10 min. RPE 1–2, Z1
2 × 10 min. RPE 7, Z4, 5 min. recovery
Cooldown: 10 min. spin
Run off the bike: 15 min.

For the run, build to RPE 5–6, Z3 and hold steady.

GETTING INTO THE BUILD PHASE HERE. INTENSITY WILL
START TO INCREASE!

TOTAL » 11 HR. 35 MIN.

LEVEL 1

	SESSION 1	SESSION 2
Mon.	**REST DAY**	
Tues.	**SWIM** **Muscular Endurance // 2300** **Warm-up:** 200 swim, 100 kick, 200 pull, all with 30 sec. rest 4 × 50 drill or stroke (no free), 15 sec. rest **Main set:** Rest 1 min. between sets: 2 × 300, 15 sec. rest 2 × 200, 15 sec. rest 2 × 100, 15 sec. rest 300 pull, focus on power, 15 sec. rest **Cooldown:** 100 easy	**RUN** **VO$_2$max Fartlek // 55 min.** **Warm-up:** 15 min. **Main set:** 10 × 90 sec. on, RPE 8, low Z5a/ 90 sec. off, RPE 5–6, Z3 **Cooldown:** 10 min. easy *Not too slow on the "off" intervals; this is very important.*
Wed.	**BRICK** **Bike Neuromuscular Power + Aerobic Run // 1 hr. 45 min.** **Warm-up:** 20 min. spin **Main set:** 60 min. RPE 5–6, Z3 with 10 sec. out-of-the-saddle bursts every 5 min., RPE 8 **Cooldown:** 10 min. spin **Run off the bike:** 15 min. RPE <4, Z1/Z2 *Shift up to two times to build speed on bursts. Keep cadence high. For the run, just find your legs and hold steady.*	
Thurs.	**SWIM** **Tri-Specific // 2600** **Warm-up:** 300 choice, 1 min. rest 6 × 50 drill, 15 sec. rest **Main set:** 200 fast, 10 sec. rest 8 × 100 at threshold, 10 sec. rest 200 fast, 2 min. rest 2 × 300 pull, 20 sec. rest **Cooldown:** 200 swim	**STRENGTH** **Pure Strength 1 // 45 min.** *See p. 252 for exercises.*

	SESSION 1	SESSION 2
Fri.	**RUN** **Neuromuscular // 30 min.** **Warm-up:** 20 min. RPE <4, Z1/Z2 **Main set:** 6 × 30 strides RPE 6, with walking recoveries **Cooldown:** 5 min. *Strides are best done on grass or soft surface. Aim for 19–20 sec. Fast but controlled.*	**BIKE** **Neuromuscular Power // 50 min.** **Warm-up:** 20 min., RPE <4, Z1/Z2 **Main set:** 8 spin-ups RPE 8, 2 min. recovery in RPE 2, Z1 **Cooldown:** 10 min. *When you start to bounce in the saddle, back off and recover. Don't push a big gear. Keep your legs sharp and increase cadence, not power.*
Sat.	**BIKE** **Lactate Threshold // 2 hr.** **Warm-up:** 15 min. RPE <4, Z1/Z2 **Main set:** 8 × 1 min. all-out, 1 min. recovery 15 min. easy spin 3 × 10 min. RPE 7, Z4, 10 min. spin recovery 15 min. tempo RPE 5–6, Z3 **Cooldown:** Spin down for the duration	**SWIM** **Aerobic Endurance Drills // 1400** **Warm-up:** 400 choice **Main set:** 8 × 50 drills for technique limiter, 20 sec. rest 6 × 50 fast with good form, 30 sec. rest **Cooldown:** 300 easy
Sun.	**BRICK** **Tempo Bike + Long Run // 2 hr. 15 min.** **Bike set:** 75 min. steady ride, RPE <6, Z1–Z3 **Run set:** 1 hr. run on rolling terrain, RPE <7, Z1–Z4 Last 15 min. of run is cooldown RPE 1–2 *Be in RPE 5–6, Z3 for at least 30 min. ahead of transition. Practice fueling.*	

THIS IS A BIG AND IMPORTANT WEEK!

TOTAL » 12 HR. 10 MIN.

LEVEL 1

	SESSION 1	SESSION 2
Mon.	**REST DAY**	

Tues.	**RUN**
	Neuromuscular // 45 min.
	Warm-up: 30 min. RPE <6, Z1–Z3
	Main set:
	6 × 200m strides with 200m jog recoveries
	Cooldown: 5 min.
	Build from slow to fast with each stride.
		SWIM
		Aerobic Endurance // 2200
		Warm-up: 200 swim, 100 kick, 200 pull, all with 30 sec. rest
		Main set:
		2 sets:
		  400 at threshold + 5 sec., 20 sec. rest
		  200 pull, aerobic, 20 sec. rest
		  200 steady kick, 30 sec. rest
		Cooldown: 100 easy

Wed.	**BIKE** **Endurance Base Building // 1 hr.** 60 min. RPE <4, Z1/Z2 *Keep cadence high.*	
Thurs.	**SWIM** **Muscular Endurance // 2900** **Warm-up:** 200 swim, 100 kick, 200 pull, all with 30 sec. rest 4 × 50 drill, 15 sec. rest **Main set:** 100 kick, 200 swim, each with 15 sec. rest 400 pull, 500 swim, 400 pull, all with 20 sec. rest 200 swim, 15 sec. rest 100 kick, 1 min. rest 4 × 25 fast, 30 sec. rest **Cooldown:** 200 easy	**STRENGTH** **Pure Strength 1 // 45 min.** *See p. 252 for exercises.*

	SESSION 1	SESSION 2
Fri.	**BIKE** **Aerobic Recovery** // **30 min.** 30 min. easy spin RPE 1–2, Z1 *Focus on smooth, even pedal stroke.*	**RUN** **Aerobic Recovery** // **20 min.** 20 min. RPE 1–2, Z1 *Controlled and relaxed.*
Sat.	**RUN** **Aerobic Long Run** // **50 min.** 50 min. *Get at least half of the time in RPE 3–4, Z2. Focus on good form and quick cadence.*	**SWIM** **Aerobic Endurance Form Work** // **1300** **Warm-up:** 200 choice **Main set:** Easy effort: 6 × 100, 30 sec. rest 2 × 200, 30 sec. rest **Cooldown:** 100 easy *Focus on form. Aim for 55–70 strokes/min.*
Sun.	**BIKE** **Endurance Recovery** // **1 hr. 20 min.** 80 min. RPE <4, Z1/Z2 *Don't exceed RPE 4, Z2 for more than a few seconds at a time as when accelerating from a stop or going up a short hill. Keep cadence comfortably high.*	

LIGHTER THIS WEEK. LET THE BIG TRAINING SINK INTO THE BODY.

TOTAL » 8 HR. 40 MIN.

	SESSION 1	SESSION 2
Mon.	**REST DAY**	

Tues.

RUN

Speed Endurance // 45 min.

Warm-up: 15 min. including strides and drills
Main set:
3 sets:
　1000m RPE 7–8, Z4/Z5a, 2 min. rest
　300m fast RPE 8+, 4 min. rest
Cooldown: 5 min.

Push the speed on the 300s.

SWIM

Muscular Endurance // 2600

Warm-up: 200 swim, 100 kick, 200 pull,
all with 30 sec. rest
4 × 50 drill, 15 sec. rest
Main set:
Rest 1 min. between sets:
3 × 300 at threshold + 10 sec., 20 sec. rest
2 × 300 at threshold, 20 sec. rest
300 pull, aerobic, 30 sec. rest
Cooldown: 100 easy

Wed.

BRICK

Bike VO₂max + Tempo Run // 1 hr. 30 min.

Warm-up: 20 min. ride
Main set:
3 sets:
　3 × 2 min. on, RPE 8+, Z5a/ 90 sec. off,
　RPE 2, Z1
　5 min. spin
Cooldown: 10 min. spin
Run off the bike: 15 min.

For the run, build to RPE 5–6, Z3 and hold steady.

Thurs.

SWIM

Tri-Specific // 2500

Warm-up: 800 choice, a mix of swim, kick,
and drills
Main set:
3 × 400 as 200 all-out/200 steady, 3 min. rest
300 pull easy
Cooldown: 200 very easy

STRENGTH

Pure Strength 1 // 45 min.

See p. 252 for exercises.

LEVEL 1

	SESSION 1	SESSION 2
Fri.	**RUN** **Neuromuscular // 30 min.** **Warm-up:** 20 min. RPE <4, Z1/Z2 **Main set:** 6 × 30 strides RPE 6, with walking recoveries **Cooldown:** 5 min. *Strides are best done on grass or soft surface. Aim for 19–20 sec. Fast but controlled.*	**BIKE** **Endurance Isolated-Leg Training // 1 hr.** **Warm-up:** 20 min. **Main set:** 20 min. as 1 min. left/1 min. right RPE 5 Get a total of 10 min. on each leg **Cooldown:** 20 min. spin *Do this on a trainer to have non-pedaling leg on a chair. Keep comfortably high cadence. Focus on eliminating dead spot in stroke by pushing toes forward in shoes at top.*
Sat.	**BIKE** **Aerobic Rolling Course // 50 min.** 50 min. RPE <6, Z1–Z3 *Focus on proud, upright form. Allow heart rate to gradually rise to RPE 6, Z3, but don't force it up.*	**SWIM** **Aerobic Endurance Drills // 1400** **Warm-up:** 400 choice **Main set:** 8 × 50 drills for technique limiter, 20 sec. rest 6 × 50 fast with good form, 30 sec. rest **Cooldown:** 300 easy
Sun.	**BRICK** **Bike Pyramid + Tempo Run // 2 hr.** **Warm-up:** 15 min. ride **Main set:** One-to-one recovery intervals after each effort: 1 min. RPE 8, Z5a, 3 min. RPE 7, Z4, 6 min. RPE 6, high Z3, 10 min. RPE 6, Z3, 6 min. RPE 6, high Z3, 3 min. RPE 7, Z4, 1 min. RPE 8, Z5a **Cooldown:** 15 min. spin **Run off the bike:** 30 min. steady *For the run, build to RPE 6, Z3 and hold steady.*	

GETTING INTO THE HIGHEST INTENSITY PHASE OF TRAINING.

TOTAL » 10 HR. 35 MIN.

LEVEL 1

	SESSION 1	SESSION 2
Mon.	**REST DAY**	

Tues.

RUN

Anaerobic Speed // 55 min.

Warm-up: 15 min.
Main set:
3 sets:
   3 × 300m RPE 8, Z5a, 1 min rest
   600m RPE 9, Z5b
Rest 4 min. between sets
Cooldown: 10 min.
Make 300s fast but controlled and 600s close to the same pace. Fast and tough!

SWIM

Muscular Endurance // 2600

Warm-up: 100 swim, 100 kick, 100 pull, all with 30 sec. rest
4 × 50 drill or stroke, 15 sec. rest
Main set:
5 × 100 free at threshold pace, 10 sec. rest
500 steady pull, 20 sec. rest
500 free at threshold pace, 20 sec. rest
5 × 100 free at threshold – 5 sec., 10 sec. rest
Cooldown: 100 easy

Wed.

BRICK

Bike Anaerobic Capacity + Tempo Run // 1 hr. 30 min.

Warm-up: 20 min. ride in RPE 1–2, Z1
Main set:
5 × 4 min. as 20 sec. on, RPE 8/
10 sec. off RPE 3–4
Spin 5 min. between sets RPE <4
Cooldown: 10 min. spin
Run off the bike: 15 min.
It's important to push very hard for the 20 sec. "on" and continue to spin lightly for the 10 sec. "off." For the run, build to RPE 6, Z3 and hold steady.

Thurs.

SWIM

Tri-Specific // 2800

Warm-up: 500 choice, a mix of swim and kick, 1 min. rest
4 × 50 drill, 15 sec. rest
Main set:
2 sets:
   4 × 50 fast, 30 sec. rest
   500 steady, 15 sec. rest
   100 kick, 1 min. rest
300 pull, 20 sec. rest
Cooldown: 200 swim

STRENGTH

Pure Strength 2 // 30 min.

See p. 252 for exercises.

	SESSION 1	SESSION 2
Fri.	**RUN**	**BIKE**
	Neuromuscular // **30 min.**	**Neuromuscular Power** // **45 min.**
	Warm-up: 20 min. RPE <4, Z1/Z2	**Warm-up:** 15 min. RPE <4, Z1/Z2
	Main set:	**Main set:**
	6 × 30 strides RPE 6, with walking recoveries	8 spin-ups RPE 8, 2 min. recovery RPE 2, Z1
	Cooldown: 5 min.	**Cooldown:** 10 min.
	Strides are best done on grass or soft surface. Aim for 19–20 sec. Fast but controlled.	*When you start to bounce in the saddle, back off and recover. Don't push a big gear. Keep your legs sharp and increase cadence, not power.*
Sat.	**BRICK**	**SWIM**
	Bike Intervals + 1000m Run // **2 hr.**	**Aerobic Endurance Drills** // **1400**
	Warm-up: 30 min. spin	**Warm-up:** 400 choice swim
	10 min. run with 4 strides	**Main set:**
	Main set:	8 × 50 drills for technique limiter, 20 sec. rest
	3 sets:	6 × 50 fast with good form, 30 sec. rest
	8 min. ride RPE 7, Z4 with 15 sec. spike into RPE 8, Z5a every 2 min.	**Cooldown:** 300 easy
	1000m run as 100m faster than race pace, building to RPE 8, Z5a/ 800m cruising at RPE 7, Z4/ 100m quick finish	
	Spin 5 min. between sets RPE 2	
	Cooldown: 10 min. easy run	
Sun.	**RUN**	
	Aerobic Base Building // **45 min.**	
	45 min. RPE <4, Z1/Z2	
	Light and easy with good form. Cadence at 90+ spm.	

TOTAL » **10 HR. 20 MIN.**

THE LEVEL 1 PROGRAM **153**

WEEK 14 ◢ BUILD 2

	SESSION 1	SESSION 2
Mon.	**REST DAY**	
Tues.	**RUN** **LTHR Test // 50 min.** *If you do not have a heart rate monitor, treat this as a benchmark test. See pp. 235–236 for details.*	**SWIM** **Aerobic Endurance // 2450** **Warm-up:** 200 swim, 100 kick, 100 pull, all with 30 sec. rest 4 × 50 drills, 15 sec. rest **Main set:** 4 × 250, 15 sec. rest 　200 swim at threshold + 5 sec. 　50 steady kick 4 × 50 fast, 30 sec. rest 4 × 25 fast, 20 sec. rest **Cooldown:** 200 choice
Wed.	**BIKE** **LTHR Test // 50 min.** *If you do not have a heart rate monitor, treat this as a benchmark test. See pp. 235–236 for details.*	
Thurs.	**SWIM** **STP Test // 2100** *See p. 234 for details.*	**STRENGTH** **Pure Strength 2 // 30 min.** *This is the last strength training session of the program. See p. 252 for exercises.*

LEVEL 1

	SESSION 1	SESSION 2
Fri.	**BRICK** **Bike Neuromuscular Power + Aerobic Run** // **50 min.** **Main set:** 40 min. ride with 5 sec. jump once every 5 min. **Run off the bike:** 10 min. RPE <4, Z1/Z2 *Ride is mostly easy, RPE <4 in Z1–Z2. Eight jumps in total, going over RPE 8, Z5a each time. For the run, just find your legs and hold steady.*	
Sat.	**SWIM** **Aerobic Endurance** // **500** *Check out the race swim venue if possible. Do 6 very short accelerations (25–50m) at race pace. Easy swimming between each for 30 sec. Be sure to check out the start and finish area. This is best done in the morning near race time.*	**BRICK** **Bike Accelerations + Run Accelerations** // **30 min.** 20 min. ride 10 min. run *Do this on the race course, if possible. Include 3–4 short, race efforts. Note landmarks. Afterward, tighten all bolts on your bike.*
Sun.	**RACE DAY!**	*You've put in some great work and have prepared properly. Now, get out, execute your race plan, and have fun!*

TOTAL » 5 HR. 10 MIN. + RACE

8

THE LEVEL 2 PROGRAM

The Level 2 Program takes you to the next level of short-course triathlon training. No longer just trying to cover the distance, Level 2 triathletes are looking to get faster and fitter. But while this plan is definitely a step up from Level 1, that doesn't mean you have to be fast or have ambitions to reach the top step of your age-group podium. What you do need to possess, however, is the will to improve and dedicate more time to the sport. If you do have ambitions of racing at a national age group or even professional level, Level 2 is an important stepping-stone before approaching the volume, intensity, and commitment of Level 3. Not only will you increase your fitness with Level 2, but you'll also learn about more advanced training techniques that will help improve your knowledge of the sport. Because you'll still be racing an event that doesn't take longer than three hours in most cases, your training volume will remain manageable in this plan, allowing for more time to hit those all-important details, such as strength training, proper stretching, and technique work. At Level 2, it's more important than ever to keep up with the supplementary work that supports your run, bike, and swim training.

LEVELING UP WITH ZONES

When you're a new triathlete, and still getting used to the sights, sounds, and sensations of multisport, we recommend training by feel. Once you've moved past the "just happy to be here" phase and into the "I want to get faster!" phase, it's still important to listen to your body, but it's also important to know that your body is sometimes an unreliable source.

As beginners, you may have relied on subjective assessments of your effort, but as you advance, it's important to transition to objective measurements as well. Your body may say, "I feel good; let's crush this workout!" because you woke up in a happy mood, when in reality your body needs rest. Your body may say, "I can't ride this fast today; my legs feel sluggish," when in fact your legs will warm up and you can do more than you'd thought. The Level 2 Program helps you get the truth out of your body by setting training zones.

Training zones are a fantastic tool to push yourself to the next level because you'll have quantifiable targets that take a lot of guesswork out of your training. While it's still very important to listen to your body (good hurt versus bad hurt, for instance), when you have a range of numbers to hit during an interval or a ceiling you cannot go above on an easy day, training

GAUGE YOUR EFFORT

In the Level 2 plan, we've included both heart-rate zones and power zones for cycling and running. While heart rate is absolutely a must-have for Level 2 training, training with power is also a very powerful tool that will help you get the most out of every session—but it requires more equipment. Training with power will give you an absolutely objective way to know how hard your muscles are working. Whichever method you choose, be sure to perform the benchmark tests throughout the plan as your heart-rate and power zones will surely change.

becomes mentally easier and more fun, giving you a numbers-based framework to build each training session around. The training equipment you'll use for these zones can even alert you when you're "in zone" with green digits, a beep, a buzz, or other notification. For anyone who's played a video game, it's like trying to get a high score by staying in zone. It can be very satisfying knowing you're training "right."

Training in zones can also be challenging. If you are used to "training by feel," you may find the experience restrictive or frustrating at first. Often it's not a matter of saying, "I can't get my heart rate high enough," but rather, "My heart rate is too high!" While a training zone will challenge you when you need to be pushed, much of that challenge involves backing off when it's time to.

Training zones provide structure, but they're not set in stone. One of the most exciting and rewarding aspects of introducing zones to your program is watching them change. Your training zones shift as your body becomes more efficient in the three sports, and as you get better at training in the correct zone. You'll actually know you're getting better when you have to adjust your zones! Changing training zones is another challenge to mitigate as a Level 2 triathlete: Make sure to follow the plan's benchmarking because if you keep your zones the same from day one all the way through to race week, you'll certainly hit a plateau. Just like growing up, as you advance as a triathlete, you'll have more responsibilities, and checking in on your zones is a big one. Let's dive in!

WEEK 1 ◢ PREP 1

	SESSION 1	SESSION 2
Mon.	**STRENGTH** **Anatomical Adaptation** // 1 hr. *See p. 252 for exercises.* *If you'd like to take one day off each week, skip the strength training on these days and take Mondays off.*	
Tues.	**RUN** **Aerobic Base Building** // 35 min. 35 min. Z1/Z2, 65–88% Run FTP *Light and easy with good form.* *Cadence at 90+ spm.*	**SWIM** **Aerobic Endurance Form Work** // 2600 **Warm-up:** 200 swim, 100 kick, 200 pull **Main set:** 4 × 200 easy, 30 sec. rest 4 × 250 easy, 30 sec. rest **Cooldown:** 6 × 50, 20 sec. rest *Focus on form. Aim for 55–70 strokes/min.*
Wed.	**BIKE** **Endurance Base Building** // 1 hr. 1 hr. Z1/Z2, 45–75% FTP *Keep cadence high.*	
Thurs.	**SWIM** **Aerobic Endurance Intervals** // 2000 **Warm-up:** 100 easy swim, 50 easy kick, 100 moderate swim, 50 moderate kick, 100 swim build speed, 50 kick build speed, all with 15 sec. rest **Main set:** 3 × 300 moderate, 10 sec. rest Rest 2 min. between sets 200 kick, steady 5 × 50 relaxed speed, 15 sec. rest **Cooldown:** 200 easy *Decrease times with each work interval for the first set.*	**STRENGTH** **Anatomical Adaptation** // 1 hr. *See p. 252 for exercises.*

	SESSION 1	SESSION 2
Fri.	**RUN**	**BIKE**
	Aerobic Recovery // 20 min.	**Aerobic Recovery // 40 min.**
	20 min. Z1, <75% Run FTP	40 min. Z1, <56% FTP
	Controlled and relaxed.	*Focus on smooth, even pedal stroke.*
Sat.	**SWIM**	**RUN**
	Aerobic Endurance Drills // 1600	**Aerobic Moderate Mid-Distance // 50 min.**
	Warm-up: 500 choice	50 min. Z1–Z3, 65–95% Run FTP
	Main set:	*Mostly Z1/Z2, <88% Run FTP. Flat to rolling terrain. Aerobic work with good form.*
	8 × 50 drills for technique limiter, 20 sec. rest	
	6 × 50 fast with good form, 30 sec. rest	
	Cooldown: 400 easy	
Sun.	**BIKE**	
	Endurance Pure Base // 1 hr. 20 min.	
	80 min. Z1–Z3, 45–80% FTP	
	It's okay to spike the power a bit into Z3 on hills or into headwinds. Mostly smooth and steady, pure base building.	

HERE WE GO! THIS PHASE IS DESIGNED TO GET YOU UP AND RUNNING. FIRST, A BUILD WEEK, THEN NEXT WEEK IS YOUR FIRST ROUND OF BASELINE TESTS.

TOTAL » 9 HR. 20 MIN.

LEVEL 2

	SESSION 1	SESSION 2
Mon.	**STRENGTH** **Anatomical Adaptation // 1 hr.** *See p. 252 for exercises.*	
Tues.	**RUN** **Test Set // 50 min.** *LTHR or RTP. See pp. 235–238 for details.*	**SWIM** **Aerobic Endurance // 2600** **Warm-up:** 200 swim, 100 kick, 200 pull, all with 30 sec. rest 6 × 50 drill, 15 sec. rest **Main set:** Rest 1 min. between sets: 6 × 150 easier than threshold, 10 sec. rest 6 × 75 easier than threshold, 10 sec. rest 4 × 25 fast, 30 sec. rest 150 kick **Cooldown:** 200 easy
Wed.	**BIKE** **FTP Test // 1 hr.** *If you do not have a power meter, do LTHR. See pp. 234–235 for details.*	
Thurs.	**SWIM** **STP Test // 2100** *See p. 234 for details.*	**STRENGTH** **Anatomical Adaptation // 1 hr.** *See p. 252 for exercises.*

	SESSION 1	SESSION 2
Fri.	**RUN**	**BIKE**
	Aerobic Recovery // **25 min.**	**Aerobic Recovery** // **30 min.**
	25 min. Z1, <75% Run FTP	30 min. easy spin Z1, <56% FTP
	Controlled and relaxed.	*Focus on a smooth, even pedal stroke.*
Sat.	**RUN**	**SWIM**
	Aerobic Moderate Mid-Distance // **1 hr. 5 min.**	**Aerobic Endurance Form Work** // **2500**
	65 min. Z1–Z3, 65–95% Run FTP	**Warm-up:** 100 swim, 100 kick, 100 pull, all with 30 sec. rest
	Mostly Z1/Z2, <88% Run FTP. Flat to rolling terrain. Aerobic work with good form.	**Main set:** Easy effort: 4 × 200, 30 sec. rest 4 × 250, 30 sec. rest
		Cooldown: 400 easy
		Focus on form. Aim for 55–70 strokes/min.
Sun.	**BIKE**	
	Endurance Pure Base // **1 hr. 35 min.**	
	95 min. Z1–Z3, 45–80% FTP	
	It's okay to spike the power a bit into Z3 on hills or into headwinds. Mostly smooth and steady, pure base building.	

TOTAL » 10 HR. 25 MIN.

	SESSION 1	SESSION 2
Mon.	**STRENGTH** **Fitness Strength // 1 hr.** *See p. 252 for exercises.*	
Tues.	**SWIM** **Aerobic Endurance // 2600** **Warm-up:** 200 swim, 100 kick, 200 pull, all with 30 sec. rest 6 × 50 drill, 15 sec. rest **Main set:** 2 sets: 　3 × 200 at threshold + 10 sec., 15 sec. rest 　100 kick, 2 min. rest 200 pull **Cooldown:** 200 choice	**RUN** **Neuromuscular // 45 min.** **Warm-up:** 35 min. Z1/Z2, 65–88% Run FTP **Main set:** 6 × 30 strides, <105% Run FTP, with walking recoveries **Cooldown:** 5 min. *Strides are best done on grass or soft surface. Aim for 19–20 sec. Fast but controlled.*
Wed.	**BRICK** **Bike Endurance Progression + Aerobic Run // 1 hr. 35 min.** **Main set:** 80 min. ride **Run off the bike:** 15 min. Z1/Z2, <88% Run FTP *First part of ride should be in Z1/Z2, 45–75% FTP. Average in Z2/Z3, 56–90% FTP, at halfway point; avoid Z4. For the run, just find your legs and hold steady.*	
Thurs.	**SWIM** **Muscular Endurance // 2800** **Warm-up:** 200 choice, 30 sec. rest 5 × 100 descend 1–5 (each set faster than previous), 30 sec. rest **Main set:** 600 steady, 30 sec. rest 500 as 75 easy/25 fast, 1 min. rest 8 × 100 race pace, 15 sec. rest **Cooldown:** 200 easy	**STRENGTH** **Fitness Strength // 1 hr.** *See p. 252 for exercises.*

	SESSION 1	SESSION 2
Fri.	**RUN** **Aerobic Recovery** // **30 min.** 30 min. Z1, <75% Run FTP *Controlled and relaxed.*	**BIKE** **Endurance Base Building** // **45 min.** 45 min. Z1/Z2, 45–75% FTP *Keep cadence high.*
Sat.	**RUN** **Aerobic Rolling Course** // **1 hr. 15 min.** 75 min. Z1–Z3, 65–95% Run FTP *Focus on proud, upright form. Allow heart rate to gradually rise to Z3, but don't force it up.*	**SWIM** **Aerobic Endurance Drills** // **1600** **Warm-up:** 500 choice of free, stroke, pull, and kick **Main set:** 8 × 50 drills for technique limiter, 20 sec. rest 6 × 50 fast with good form, 30 sec. rest **Cooldown:** 400 easy
Sun.	**BIKE** **Endurance Cadence Drills** // **1 hr. 45 min.** **Warm-up:** 45 min. **Main set:** 6 × 1 min. on/1 min. off 10 min. spin 2 × 5 min. on/5 min. off 2 × 1 min. on/1 min. off **Cooldown:** 14 min. *1 min. intervals: Z3/Z4, 76–105% FTP.* *5 min. intervals: 100 rpm Z3, 76–90% FTP.* *Spin in Z1, <56% FTP, for "off" intervals.*	

STARTING TO BUILD SOME GOOD BASE!

TOTAL » 10 HR. 45 MIN.

LEVEL 2

	SESSION 1	SESSION 2
Mon.	**STRENGTH** **Fitness Strength** // 1 hr. *See p. 252 for exercises.*	

Tues.	**RUN**
	Neuromuscular // 55 min.
	Warm-up: 40 min. Z1–Z3, 65–95% Run FTP
	Main set:
	6 × 200m strides, <105% Run FTP, with 200m jog recoveries
	Cooldown: 5 min.
	Build from slow to fast with each stride set.
		SWIM
		Aerobic Endurance // 2800
		Warm-up: 200 swim, 100 kick, 200 pull, all with 30 sec. rest
		6 × 50 drill or stroke (no free), 15 sec. rest
		Main set:
		3 sets:
		   500 free at 100 threshold pace + 5 sec., 20 sec. rest
		   100 kick, 30 sec. rest
		Cooldown: 200 easy

Wed.	**BRICK** **Tempo Bike + Aerobic Run** // 1 hr. 45 min. **Warm-up:** 30 min. ride **Main set:** 45 min. Z3, 76–90% FTP **Cooldown:** 15 min. spin **Run off the bike:** 20 min. Z1/Z2, 65–88% Run FTP *For the run, just find your legs and hold steady.*	

Thurs.	**SWIM**
	Muscular Endurance // 3000
	Warm-up: 200 swim, 100 kick, 200 pull, all with 30 sec. rest
	8 × 50 drill, 15 sec. rest
	Main set:
	Swims at 100 threshold pace + 5 sec.
	   500 free, 400 pull, each with 20 sec. rest
	   300 free, 200 kick, each with 15 sec. rest
	100 free fast, 1 min. rest
	4 × 100 at threshold, 10 sec. rest
	Cooldown: 200 swim
		STRENGTH
		Fitness Strength // 1 hr.
		See p. 252 for exercises.

	SESSION 1	SESSION 2
Fri.	**RUN** **Aerobic Base Building** // 30 min. 30 min. Z1/Z2, 65–88% Run FTP *Light and easy with good form.* *Cadence at 90+ spm.*	**BIKE** **Endurance Base Building** // 50 min. 50 min. Z1/Z2, 45–75% FTP *Keep cadence high.*
Sat.	**RUN** **Aerobic Rolling Course** // 1 hr. 25 min. 85 min. Z1–Z3, 65–95% Run FTP *Focus on proud, upright form. Allow heart rate to gradually rise to Z3, but don't force it up.*	**SWIM** **Aerobic Endurance Drills** // 1600 **Warm-up:** 500 choice **Main set:** 8 × 50 drills for technique limiter, 20 sec. rest 6 × 50 fast with good form, 30 sec. rest **Cooldown:** 400 easy
Sun.	**BRICK** **Endurance Bike + Aerobic Run** // **2 hr. 20 min.** **Warm-up:** 30 min. ride **Main set:** 90 min. Z2/Z3, 56–90% FTP, with 8 sec. bursts to Z7, 150% FTP, every 10 min. **Cooldown:** 15 min. spin **Run off the bike:** 20 min. Z1/Z2, 65–88% Run FTP *Relatively high cadence for the bike warm-up (90 rpm). Bursts should be 80% of a full sprint, 105+ rpm. For the run, just find your legs and hold steady.*	

TOTAL » 12 HR. 50 MIN.

WEEK 5 ◢ BASE 1

PHASE 2

	SESSION 1	SESSION 2
Mon.	**REST DAY**	

LEVEL 2

Tues.

SWIM

Aerobic Endurance // 2300

Warm-up: 200 swim, 100 kick, 200 pull, all with 30 sec. rest
6 × 50 drill, 15 sec. rest
Main set:
2 sets:
   300 swim at threshold + 5 sec., 15 sec. rest
   200 steady swim at threshold + 5 sec., 15 sec. rest
   100 fast, 1 min. rest
100 kick
Cooldown: 200 swim

RUN

Aerobic Moderate Mid-Distance // 45 min.

45 min. Z1–Z3, 65–95% Run FTP

Mostly Z1/Z2, <75% Run FTP. Flat to rolling terrain. Aerobic work with good form.

Wed.

BIKE

Neuromuscular Power // 1 hr.

Warm-up: 30 min. Z1/Z2, 45–75% FTP
Main set:
8 spin-ups, 2 min. recovery
Cooldown: 10 min. spin

When you start to bounce in the saddle, back off and recover. Don't push a big gear. Keep your legs sharp and increase cadence, not power.

Thurs.

SWIM

Muscular Endurance // 2400

Warm-up: 200 swim, 100 kick, 200 pull, all with 30 sec. rest
4 × 50 drill, 15 sec. rest
Main set:
4 × 250 as 100 moderate/50 build/100 moderate, 20 sec. rest
1 min. rest
500 with second 250 10 sec. faster than first, 30 sec. rest
1 min. rest
Cooldown: 200 swim

STRENGTH

Fitness Strength // 1 hr.

See p. 252 for exercises.

	SESSION 1	SESSION 2
Fri.	**RUN** **Aerobic Recovery** // 20 min. 20 min. Z1, <75% Run FTP *Controlled and relaxed.*	**BIKE** **Aerobic Recovery** // 40 min. 40 min. Z1, <56% FTP *Focus on smooth, even pedal stroke.*
Sat.	**RUN** **Aerobic Long Run** // 1 hr. 10 min. 70 min. *Get at least half of the time in Z2, 76–88% Run FTP. Focus on good form and quick cadence.*	**SWIM** **Aerobic Endurance Form Work** // 2700 **Warm-up:** 400 choice 6 × 50 drill, 15 sec. rest. **Main set:** Easy effort: 4 × 200, 30 sec. rest 4 × 250, 30 sec. rest **Cooldown:** 100 kick, 100 swim *Focus on form. Aim for 55–70 strokes/min.*
Sun.	**BIKE** **Endurance Recovery** // 1 hr. 20 min. 80 min. Z1/Z2, <75% FTP *Don't exceed Z2 for more than a few seconds at a time as when accelerating from a stop or going up a short hill. Comfortably high rpm.*	

LIGHTER THIS WEEK. LET THE BODY AND MIND RECOVER
FROM THE LAST TWO WEEKS OF SOLID BASE BUILDING.

TOTAL » 9 HR. 20 MIN.

WEEK 6 ◢ BASE 2

	SESSION 1	SESSION 2
Mon.	**STRENGTH** **Fitness Strength // 1 hr.** *See p. 252 for exercises.*	
Tues.	**RUN** **Tempo // 1 hr.** **Warm-up:** 20 min. Z1/Z2, 65–88% Run FTP **Main set:** 20 min. Z2/Z3, 76–95% Run FTP 20 min. steady Z3, 89–95% Run FTP *Pace and heart rate should progressively increase as the run progresses.*	**SWIM** **Muscular Endurance // 2600** **Warm-up:** 200 swim, 100 kick, 200 pull, all with 30 sec. rest; 6 × 50 drill, 15 sec. rest **Main set:** 300 swim, 300 pull, each with 15 sec. rest 100 fast swim, 1 min. rest 200 swim, 200 pull, each with 15 sec. rest 100 fast swim, 1 min. rest 100 swim, 100 pull, each with 15 sec. rest 100 fast swim, 1 min. rest; 100 kick, 15 sec. rest **Cooldown:** 200 choice
Wed.	**BRICK** **Bike Power Development + Aerobic Run // 1 hr. 30 min.** **Warm-up:** 20 min. ride **Main set:** 3 min. at 40 rpm, 2 min. recovery 6 min. at 50 rpm, 3 min. recovery 12 min. at 60 rpm, 4 min. recovery 6 min. at 50 rpm, 3 min. recovery 3 min. at 40 rpm, 2 min. recovery **Cooldown:** 11 min. very easy spin **Run off the bike:** 15 min. Z1/Z2, <88% Run FTP *Bike recoveries should all be in Z1, <56% FTP, at a cadence of 80–100 rpm. Intervals should go from low Z4, <95% FTP, in the shortest sets to Z3, <90% FTP, in the longest. For the run, just find your legs and hold steady.*	
Thurs.	**SWIM** **Threshold // 3200** **Warm-up:** 200 swim, 100 kick, 200 pull, all with 30 sec. rest 4 × 50 drill, 15 sec. rest **Main set:** Rest 30 sec. between sets: 3 × 350 swim/pull/swim at threshold, 15 sec. rest 3 × 250 swim/pull/swim at threshold, 15 sec. rest 3 × 150 swim/pull/swim at threshold, 15 sec. rest 3 × 50 swim/pull/swim at threshold, 20 sec. rest **Cooldown:** 100 swim	**STRENGTH** **Fitness Strength // 1 hr.** *See p. 252 for exercises.*

	SESSION 1	SESSION 2
Fri.	**RUN** **Neuromuscular** // **30 min.** **Warm-up:** 20 min. Z1/Z2, 65–88% Run FTP **Main set:** 6 × 30 strides, >105% Run FTP, with walking recoveries **Cooldown:** 5 min. *Strides are best done on grass or soft surface. Aim for 19–20 sec. Fast but controlled.*	**BIKE** **Endurance Base Building** // **50 min.** 50 min. Z1/Z2, 45–75% FTP *Keep cadence high.*

Sat.	**RUN**
	
	Long Run // **1 hr. 20 min.**
	
	80 min.
	
	The first 50 min. of the run are all aerobic in Z1 and Z2. Tempo finish, last 30 min. in Z3. Relax! Record your tempo pace during the last 30 min.
		SWIM
		
		Muscular Endurance // **2500**
		
		Warm-up: 100 swim, 100 stroke, 100 kick, all with 30 sec. rest
		4 × 50 drill or stroke, 15 sec. rest
		Main set:
		Swims at 100 threshold + 5 sec. with 20 sec. rest post kick or pull:
		    100 swim, 50 kick; 200 swim, 50 kick
		    300 swim, 50 kick; 400 pull
		    300 swim, 50 kick; 200 swim, 50 kick
		    100 swim, 50 kick
		Cooldown: 100 easy

Sun.	**BRICK** **Bike Endurance Intervals + Aerobic Run** // **2 hr. 30 min.** **Warm-up:** 30 min. ride **Main set:** 5 × 1 min. primer repeats, 2 min. recovery 4 × 15 min. repeats, 5 min. recovery **Cooldown:** 10 min. spin **Run off the bike:** 15 min. Z1/Z2, 65–88% Run FTP *Primer repeats in Z3/Z4, 76–105% FTP. 15 min. repeats in Z3, 76–90% FTP. This should feel smooth and steady. Lock in the pace and hold. For the run, just find your legs and hold steady.*	**SWIM** **Aerobic Endurance Drills** // **1400** **Warm-up:** 500 choice **Main set:** 8 × 50 drills for technique limiter, 20 sec. rest 6 × 50 fast with good form, 30 sec. rest **Cooldown:** 200 easy

GETTING IN SOME MORE BASE WORK. VOLUME WILL CONTINUE TO INCREASE, AND INTENSITY WILL RISE JUST A BIT TOO. THERE'S ALSO AN ADDED SWIM EACH WEEK.

TOTAL » 13 HR. 45 MIN.

WEEK 7 ◢ BASE 2

PHASE 2

LEVEL 2

	SESSION 1	SESSION 2
Mon.	**STRENGTH** **Fitness Strength** // 1 hr. *See p. 252 for exercises.*	
Tues.	**RUN** **Speed Strength** // 1 hr. 5 min. **Warm-up:** 30 min. moderate **Main set:** 10 × 80m hill sprints Jog downhill for recovery 2 miles Z4+ **Cooldown:** 5 min. jog *Do the hill sprints on a 6–10% grade.* *Fast and powerful. 2-mile run is at tempo pace.*	**SWIM** **Muscular Endurance** // 3000 **Warm-up:** 200 swim, 100 kick, 200 pull, all with 30 sec. rest 8 × 50 drill or stroke (no free), 15 sec. rest **Main set:** 3 × 300 steady pull, 15 sec. rest 4 × 150 threshold swim, 10 sec. rest 6 × 50 speed swim, 30 sec. rest 100 easy kick **Cooldown:** 200 choice
Wed.	**BRICK** **Bike Power Development +** **Aerobic Run** // 1 hr. 45 min. **Warm-up:** 20 min. ride **Main set:** 6 × 5 min. at 55 rpm Z4, 91–105% FTP, 5 min. recovery **Cooldown:** 10 min. spin **Run off the bike:** 15 min. Z1/Z2, 65–88% Run FTP *Do bike intervals on flat or slightly uphill terrain.* *Constant pressure on the pedals. For the run,* *just find your legs and hold steady.*	

Thurs.	**SWIM**
	Threshold // 3000
	Warm-up: 200 swim, 100 kick, 200 pull,
	all with 30 sec. rest
	6 × 50 drill or stroke (no free), 15 sec. rest
	Main set:
	2 sets:
	   300 steady pull, 20 sec. rest
	   5 × 100 at threshold, 10 sec. rest
	1 min. rest
	300 pull, 30 sec. rest
	100 easy kick
	Cooldown: 200 easy
		STRENGTH
		Fitness Strength // 1 hr.
		See p. 252 for exercises.

	SESSION 1	SESSION 2
Fri.	**RUN**	**BIKE**
	Neuromuscular // 30 min.	**Endurance Base Building** // 50 min.
	Warm-up: 20 min. Z1/Z2, 65–88% Run FTP	50 min. Z1/Z2, 45–75% FTP
	Main set:	*Keep cadence high.*
	6 × 30 strides, >105% Run FTP, with walking recoveries	
	Cooldown: 5 min.	
	Strides are best done on grass or soft surface. Aim for 19–20 sec. Fast but controlled.	
Sat.	**RUN**	**SWIM**
	Long Run // 1 hr. 30 min.	**Aerobic Endurance** // 2900
	Warm-up: 20 min.	**Warm-up:** 200 swim, 100 kick, 200 pull, each with 30 sec. rest
	Main set:	4 × 50 drill, 15 sec. rest
	60 min. Z3, 89–95% Run FTP	**Main set:**
	Cooldown: 10 min.	Swims at threshold + 5 sec. per 100
	Focus on good form with 90+ spm cadence.	4 × 200, 15 sec. rest
		4 × 150, 15 sec. rest
		4 × 100, 15 sec. rest
		4 × 50 fast, 30 sec. rest
		Cooldown: 200 choice
Sun.	**BRICK**	**SWIM**
	Endurance Bike + Aerobic Run // 3 hr. 15 min.	**Aerobic Endurance Drills** // 1400
	Main set:	**Warm-up:** 500 choice
	3 hr. ride Z1/Z2, 45–75% FTP	**Main set:**
	Run off the bike: 15 min.	8 × 50 drills for technique limiter, 20 sec. rest
	Ride should mostly be in Z1/Z2. Okay to spike into Z3, <90% FTP, every once in a while. Plan accordingly with nutrition and hydration.	6 × 50 fast with good form, 30 sec. rest
		Cooldown: 200 easy

TOTAL » **15 HR. 10 MIN.**

WEEK 8 ◢ BASE 2

PHASE 2

LEVEL 2

	SESSION 1	SESSION 2
Mon.	**REST DAY**	
Tues.	**RUN** **Test Set** // 50 min. *LTHR or RTP. See pp. 235–238 for details.*	**SWIM** **Muscular Endurance** // 2300 **Warm-up:** 200 swim, 100 kick, 200 pull, all with 30 sec. rest; 4 × 50 drill, 15 sec. rest **Main set:** 300 swim, 300 pull; each with 15 sec. rest 100 fast swim, 1 min. rest 200 swim, 200 pull; each with 15 sec. rest 100 fast swim, 1 min. rest 100 swim, 100 pull; each with 15 sec. rest 100 fast swim **Cooldown:** 100 choice
Wed.	**BIKE** **FTP Test** // 1 hr. *If you do not have a power meter, do LTHR. See pp. 234–235 for details.*	
Thurs.	**SWIM** **STP Test** // 2100 *See p. 234 for details.*	**STRENGTH** **Fitness Strength** // 1 hr. *See p. 252 for exercises.*

	SESSION 1	SESSION 2
Fri.	**RUN** **Aerobic Recovery** // 20 min. 20 min. Z1, <75% Run FTP *Controlled and relaxed.*	**BIKE** **Aerobic Recovery** // 30 min. 30 min. Z1, <56% FTP *Focus on smooth, even pedal stroke.*
Sat.	**RUN** **Aerobic Long Run** // 1 hr. 60 min. *Get at least half of the time in Z2, 76–88% Run FTP. Focus on good form and quick cadence.*	**SWIM** **Aerobic Endurance Form Work** // 1800 **Warm-up:** 300 choice **Main set:** Easy effort: 6 × 100, 30 sec. rest 4 × 200, 30 sec. rest **Cooldown:** 100 easy *Focus on form. Aim for 55–70 strokes/min.*
Sun.	**BIKE** **Endurance Recovery** // 1 hr. 20 min. 80 min. Z1/Z2, <75% FTP *Don't exceed Z2 for more than a few seconds at a time as when accelerating from a stop or going up a short hill. Comfortably high rpm.*	

BACKING OFF THE TRAINING A BIT AND GETTING IN SOME CHECK–IN TESTS. AFTER EACH TEST, YOU'LL NEED TO MODIFY YOUR TRAINING ZONES.

TOTAL » 8 HR. 40 MIN.

LEVEL 2

	SESSION 1	SESSION 2
Mon.	**STRENGTH** **Pure Strength 1 // 45 min.** *See p. 252 for exercises.*	
Tues.	**SWIM** **Muscular Endurance // 2900** **Warm-up:** 200 swim, 100 kick, 200 pull, all with 30 sec. rest 4 × 50 drill, 15 sec. rest **Main set:** 100 kick, 200 swim, each with 15 sec. rest 400 pull, 500 swim, 400 pull, all with 20 sec. rest 200 swim, 15 sec. rest 100 kick, 1 min. rest 4 × 25 fast, 30 sec. rest **Cooldown:** 200 easy	**RUN** **Speed Strength // 1 hr.** **Warm-up:** 15 min. **Main set:** 5 × 800m uphill run Jog downhill between each one **Cooldown:** 10 min. easy *Hill should be 4–6% grade. Build to Z4, 96–104% Run FTP, on each set. Focus on driving the legs and arms up the hill.*
Wed.	**BRICK** **Bike Neuromuscular Power + Aerobic Run // 1 hr. 30 min.** **Warm-up:** 20 min. ride **Main set:** 3 sets: 10 min. of 15 sec. on/15 sec. off Spin 5 min. between sets **Cooldown:** 10 min. ride **Run off the bike:** 15 min. Z1/Z2, <88% Run FTP *On the bike, 15-sec. "on" intervals are >150% FTP, "off" intervals are easy spin. For the run, just find your legs and hold steady.*	

Thurs.	**SWIM**
	
	Tri-Specific // 2900
	
	Warm-up: 200 swim, 100 kick, 200 pull, all with 30 sec. rest
	6 × 50 drill or stroke (no free), 15 sec. rest
	Main set:
	2 sets:
	  200 fast, 10 sec. rest
	  300 steady swim, 15 sec. rest
	  400 pull, 30 sec. rest
	8 × 25 fast, 30 sec. rest
	Cooldown: 100 easy
		STRENGTH
		
		Pure Strength 1 // 45 min.
		
		See p. 252 for exercises.

	SESSION 1	SESSION 2
Fri.	**RUN** **Neuromuscular** // 30 min. **Warm-up:** 20 min. Z1/Z2, 65–88% Run FTP **Main set:** 6 × 30 strides, >105% Run FTP, with walking recoveries **Cooldown:** 5 min. *Strides are best done on grass or soft surface. Aim for 19–20 sec. Fast but controlled.*	**BIKE** **Endurance Isolated-Leg Training** // 50 min. **Warm-up:** 20 min. **Main set:** 20 min. as 1 min. left/1 min. right Get a total of 10 min. on each leg **Cooldown:** 10 min. spin *Do this on a trainer to have non-pedaling leg on a chair. Keep comfortably high cadence. Focus on eliminating dead spot in stroke by pushing toes forward in shoes at top.*

Sat.	**RUN**
	
	Long Run // 1 hr. 25 min.
	
	Warm-up: 25 min.
	Main set:
	5 sets:
	    1200m Z4, 96–104% Run FTP
	    400m jog
	Cooldown: Z1 jog for duration, <75% Run FTP
	
	This should be high quality. Focus on good efforts during the 1200s.
		SWIM
		
		Threshold // 2700
		
		Warm-up: 500 choice, 1 min. rest;
		4 × 50 drills, 15 sec. rest
		Main set:
		4 × 200, 20 sec. rest
		1 min. rest
		4 × 100, 20 sec. rest
		1 min. rest
		400 steady pull
		30 sec. rest
		4 × 25 fast, 30 sec. rest; 100 easy kick
		Cooldown: 200 choice

Sun.	**BRICK** **Tempo Bike + Tempo Run** // 2 hr. 30 min. **Warm-up:** 40 min. ride **Main set:** 45 min. tempo, 76–90% FTP 10 min. Z1, <56% FTP 2 × 10 min. Z4, 91–105% FTP, 5 min. recovery **Cooldown:** 10 min. spin **Run off the bike:** 15 min. *For the run, build to Z3, 89–95% Run FTP, and hold steady.*	**SWIM** **Aerobic Endurance Drills** // 1400 **Warm-up:** 400 choice **Main set:** 8 × 50 drills for technique limiter, 20 sec. rest 6 × 50 fast with good form, 30 sec. rest **Cooldown:** 300 easy

GETTING INTO THE BUILD PHASE HERE. INTENSITY WILL START TO INCREASE!

TOTAL » 13 HR. 25 MIN.

LEVEL 2

	SESSION 1	SESSION 2
Mon.	**STRENGTH** **Pure Strength 1 // 45 min.** *See p. 252 for exercises.*	
Tues.	**SWIM** **Muscular Endurance // 3300** **Warm-up:** 200 swim, 100 kick, 200 pull, all with 30 sec. rest 4 × 50 drill or stroke (no free), 15 sec. rest **Main set:** Rest 1 min. between sets: 3 × 300, 15 sec. rest 3 × 200, 15 sec. rest 3 × 100, 15 sec. rest 3 × 200 pull, focus on power, 15 sec. rest **Cooldown:** 200 easy	**RUN** **VO$_2$max Fartlek // 1 hr.** **Warm-up:** 20 min. at <110% Run FTP easy **Main set:** 10 × 90 sec. on, low Z5a, <110% Run FTP/ 90 sec. off, Z3, 89–95% Run FTP **Cooldown:** 10 min. easy *Not too slow on the "off" intervals; this is very important.*
Wed.	**BRICK** **Bike Neuromuscular Power + Aerobic Run // 1 hr. 45 min.** **Warm-up:** 20 min. spin **Main set:** 60 min. Z3, 76–90% FTP, with 10 sec. out-of-the-saddle bursts every 5 min., >150% FTP **Cooldown:** 10 min. spin **Run off the bike:** 15 min. Z1/Z2, <88% Run FTP *Shift up to two times to build speed on bursts. Keep cadence high. For the run, just find your legs and hold steady.*	
Thurs.	**SWIM** **Tri-Specific // 3000** **Warm-up:** 400 choice, 1 min. rest 6 × 50 drill, 15 sec. rest **Main set:** 200 fast, 10 sec. rest 8 × 100 at threshold, 10 sec. rest 200 fast, 2 min. rest 3 × 300 pull, 20 sec. rest **Cooldown:** 200 easy	**STRENGTH** **Pure Strength 1 // 45 min.** *See p. 252 for exercises.*

	SESSION 1	SESSION 2
Fri.	**RUN** **Neuromuscular // 30 min.** **Warm-up:** 20 min. Z1/Z2, 65–88% Run FTP **Main set:** 6 × 30 strides, >105% Run FTP, with walking recoveries **Cooldown:** 5 min. *Strides are best done on grass or soft surface. Aim for 19–20 sec. Fast but controlled.*	**BIKE** **Neuromuscular Power // 50 min.** **Warm-up:** 20 min. Z1/Z2, 45–75% FTP **Main set:** 8 spin-ups, 2 min. recovery **Cooldown:** 10 min. spin *When you start to bounce in the saddle, back off and recover. Don't push a big gear. Keep your legs sharp and increase cadence, not power.*
Sat.	**BIKE** **Lactate Threshold // 2 hr. 30 min.** **Warm-up:** 20 min. Z1/Z2, 45–75% FTP **Main set:** 8 × 1 min. all-out, >150% FTP, 1 min. recovery 15 min. spin 2 × 10 min. Z4, 91–105% FTP, 10 min. spin recovery 30 min. tempo Z3, 76–90% FTP **Cooldown:** Spin for the duration	**SWIM** **Threshold // 2400** **Warm-up:** 200 swim, 100 kick, 200 pull, all with 30 sec. rest 4 × 50 drill, 15 sec. rest **Main set:** 3 × 500 at threshold pace, 45 sec. rest **Cooldown:** 200 swim *Perfect form on the cooldown.*
Sun.	**BRICK** **Tempo Bike + Long Run // 2 hr. 15 min.** **Bike set:** 75 min. steady ride, Z1–Z3, 45–90% FTP **Run set:** 1 hr. run on rolling terrain, Z1–Z4, <104% Run FTP. Last 15 min. of run are cooldown *Be in Z3, 76–90% FTP, for at least 30 min. ahead of transition. Practice fueling.*	**SWIM** **Aerobic Endurance Drills // 1500** **Warm-up:** 500 choice **Main set:** 8 × 50 drills for technique limiter, 20 sec. rest 6 × 50 fast with good form, 30 sec. rest **Cooldown:** 300 easy

THIS IS A BIG AND IMPORTANT WEEK!

TOTAL » 14 HR. 35 MIN.

LEVEL 2

	SESSION 1	SESSION 2
Mon.	**REST DAY**	
Tues.	**RUN** **Neuromuscular // 50 min.** **Warm-up:** 35 min. Z1–Z3, 65–95% Run FTP **Main set:** 6 × 200m strides, <105% Run FTP, with 200m jog recoveries **Cooldown:** 5 min. *Build from slow to fast with each stride set.*	**SWIM** **Aerobic Endurance // 2300** **Warm-up:** 500 easy mix of swim and kick **Main set:** 2 sets: 400 free at threshold + 5 sec., 20 sec. rest 200 pull, aerobic, 20 sec. rest 200 steady kick, 30 sec. rest **Cooldown:** 200 easy
Wed.	**BIKE** **Endurance Base Building // 1 hr. 10 min.** 70 min. Z1/Z2, 45–75% FTP *Keep cadence high.*	
Thurs.	**SWIM** **Muscular Endurance // 3000** **Warm-up:** 200 swim, 100 kick, 200 pull, all with 30 sec. rest 4 × 50 drill, 15 sec. rest **Main set:** 100 kick, 200 swim, each with 15 sec. rest 400 pull, 500 swim, 400 pull, all with 20 sec. rest 200 swim, 15 sec. rest 100 kick, 1 min. rest 8 × 25 fast, 30 sec. rest **Cooldown:** 200 easy	**STRENGTH** **Pure Strength 1 // 45 min.** *See p. 252 for exercises.*

	SESSION 1	SESSION 2
Fri.	**BIKE** **Aerobic Recovery** // **30 min.** 30 min. easy spin Z1, <56% FTP *Focus on smooth, even pedal stroke.*	**RUN** **Aerobic Recovery** // **20 min.** 20 min. Z1, <75% Run FTP *Controlled and relaxed.*
Sat.	**RUN** **Aerobic Long Run** // **1 hr.** 60 min. *Get at least half of the time in Z2, 76–88% Run FTP.* *Focus on good form and quick cadence.*	**SWIM** **Aerobic Endurance Form Work** // **1900** **Warm-up:** 300 choice, mix of swim and kick **Main set:** Easy effort: 6 × 100 easy, 30 sec. rest 4 × 200 easy, 30 sec. rest **Cooldown:** 200 easy *Focus on form. Aim for 55–70 strokes/min.*
Sun.	**BIKE** **Endurance Recovery** // **1 hr. 25 min.** 85 min. Z1/Z2, <75% FTP *Don't exceed Z2 for more than a few seconds* *at a time as when accelerating from a stop* *or going up a short hill. Comfortably high rpm.*	

LIGHTER THIS WEEK. LET THE BIG TRAINING SINK INTO THE BODY.

TOTAL » 9 HR.

	SESSION 1	SESSION 2
Mon.	**STRENGTH** **Pure Strength 1 // 45 min.** *See p. 252 for exercises.*	

Tues.	**RUN**
	Speed Endurance // 1 hr.
	Warm-up: 15 min. including strides and drills
	Main set:
	4 sets:
	   1000m high Z4/low Z5a, 100–110% Run FTP, 2 min. rest
	   300m fast, 4 min. rest
	Cooldown: 10 min.
	Don't worry about zones on the 300s, just push the speed.
		SWIM
		Muscular Endurance // 3300
		Warm-up: 200 swim, 100 kick, 200 pull, all with 30 sec. rest
		4 × 50 drill, 15 sec. rest
		Main set:
		Rest 1 min. between sets:
		3 × 300 at threshold + 15 sec., 15 sec. rest
		3 × 300 at threshold, 15 sec. rest
		2 × 300 at threshold − 10 sec., 15 sec. rest
		Cooldown: 200 choice

Wed.	**BRICK**
	Bike VO$_2$max + Tempo Run // 1 hr. 35 min.
	Warm-up: 20 min. ride
	Main set:
	3 sets:
	   3 × 2 min. on/90 sec. off
	   5 min. spin
	Cooldown: 15 min. spin
	Run off the bike: 15 min.
	On the bike, 2-min. "on" intervals Z5a, 121–150% FTP, then recover in Z1, <56% FTP; "off" intervals spin in Z1, <56% FTP. Set rests are also spin at Z1. For the run, build to Z3, 89–95% Run FTP, and hold steady.	

Thurs.	**SWIM** **Tri-Specific // 2600** **Warm-up:** 800 choice, a mix of swim, kick, and drills **Main set:** 3 × 400 as 200 all-out/200 steady, 3 min. rest 400 pull easy **Cooldown:** 200 very easy	**STRENGTH** **Pure Strength 1 // 45 min.** *See p. 252 for exercises.*

	SESSION 1	SESSION 2
Fri.	**RUN** **Neuromuscular // 30 min.** **Warm-up:** 20 min. Z1/Z2, 65–88% Run FTP **Main set:** 6 × 30 strides, >105% Run FTP, with walking recoveries **Cooldown:** 5 min. *Strides are best done on grass or soft surface. Aim for 19–20 sec. Fast but controlled.*	**BIKE** **Endurance Isolated-Leg Training // 1 hr.** **Warm-up:** 20 min. **Main set:** 20 min. as 1 min. left/1 min. right Get a total of 10 min. on each leg **Cooldown:** 20 min. spin *Do this on a trainer to have non-pedaling leg on a chair. Keep comfortably high cadence. Focus on eliminating dead spot in stroke by pushing toes forward in shoes at top.*
Sat.	**RUN** **Aerobic Rolling Course // 1 hr.** 60 min. Z1–Z3, 65–95% Run FTP *Focus on proud, upright form. Allow heart rate to gradually rise to Z3, but don't force it up.*	**SWIM** **Aerobic Endurance // 2700** **Warm-up:** 200 swim, 200 stroke (no free), 200 kick, all with 30 sec. rest **Main set:** 6 × 200 as 150 swim at threshold + 5 sec. per 100/50 kick, 10 sec. rest 2 min. rest 4 × 200 pull at threshold + 5 sec. per 100, 15 sec. rest **Cooldown:** 100 easy
Sun.	**BRICK** **Bike Pyramid + Tempo Run // 2 hr. 15 min.** **Warm-up:** 30 min. ride **Main set:** One-to-one recovery intervals after each effort: 3 min. Z4, 91–105% FTP 6 min. high Z3, 80–90% FTP 12 min. Z3, 76–90% FTP 6 min. high Z3, 80–90% FTP 3 min. Z4, 91–105% FTP **Cooldown:** 15 min. spin **Run off the bike:** 30 min. steady *For the run, build to Z3, 89–95% Run FTP, and hold steady.*	**SWIM** **Aerobic Endurance Drills // 1400** **Warm-up:** 400 choice, a mix of swim, pull, and kick **Main set:** 8 × 50 drills for technique limiter, 20 sec. rest 6 × 50 fast with good form, 30 sec. rest **Cooldown:** 300 easy

GETTING INTO THE HIGHEST INTENSITY PHASE OF TRAINING.

TOTAL » 13 HR.

LEVEL 2

	SESSION 1	SESSION 2
Mon.	**STRENGTH** **Pure Strength 2 // 30 min.** *See p. 252 for exercises.*	

Tues.	**RUN**
	
	Anaerobic Speed // 55 min.
	
	Warm-up: 15 min.
	Main set:
	3 sets:
	    3 × 300m Z5a, 105–114% Run FTP, 1 min rest
	    600m Z5a–Z5b, 105–125% Run FTP
	Rest 4 min. between sets
	Cooldown: 10 min.
	
	Make 300s fast but controlled and 600s close to the same pace. Fast and tough!
		SWIM
		
		Muscular Endurance // 2800
		
		Warm-up: 200 swim, 100 kick, 200 pull, all with 30 sec. rest
		4 × 50 drill or stroke, 15 sec. rest
		Main set:
		5 × 100 free at threshold pace, 10 sec. rest
		500 steady pull, 20 sec. rest
		500 free at threshold pace, 20 sec. rest
		5 × 100 free at threshold — 5 sec., 10 sec. rest
		Cooldown: 100 easy

Wed.	**BRICK** **Bike Anaerobic Capacity + Tempo Run // 1 hr. 30 min.** **Warm-up:** 20 min. ride Z1, <56% FTP **Main set:** 5 × 4 min. as 20 sec. on/10 sec. off Spin 5 min. between sets **Cooldown:** 10 min. spin **Run off the bike:** 15 min. *It's important to push very hard, 121–150+% FTP, for the 20 sec. "on" and continue to spin lightly for the 10 sec. "off." For the run, build to Z3, 89–95% Run FTP, and hold steady.*	

Thurs.	**SWIM**
	
	Tri-Specific // 2900
	
	Warm-up: 600 choice, a mix of swim and kick, 1 min. rest
	4 × 50 drill, 15 sec. rest
	Main set:
	2 sets:
	    4 × 50 fast, 30 sec. rest
	    500 steady, 15 sec. rest
	    100 kick, 1 min. rest
	300 pull, 20 sec. rest
	Cooldown: 200 swim
		STRENGTH
		
		Pure Strength 2 // 30 min.
		
		See p. 252 for exercises.

	SESSION 1	SESSION 2
Fri.	**RUN** **Neuromuscular** // **30 min.** **Warm-up:** 20 min. Z1/Z2, 65–88% Run FTP **Main set:** 6 × 30 strides, >105% Run FTP, with walking recoveries **Cooldown:** 5 min. *Strides are best done on grass or soft surface. Aim for 19–20 sec. Fast but controlled.*	**BIKE** **Neuromuscular Power** // **50 min.** **Warm-up:** 20 min. Z1/Z2, 45–75% FTP **Main set:** 8 spin-ups, 2 min. recovery **Cooldown:** 10 min. spin *When you start to bounce in the saddle, back off and recover. Don't push a big gear. Keep your legs sharp and increase cadence, not power.*

Sat.	**BRICK**
	
	Bike Intervals + 1200m Run // **2 hr. 10 min.**
	
	Warm-up: 30 min. spin
	15 min. run with 4 sets of strides
	Main set:
	3 sets:
	  10 min. ride Z4, 91–105% FTP, with 15 sec. spike into Z5a, >106% FTP, every 2 min.
	  1200m run as 200m faster than race pace, building to Z5a, 105–114% Run FTP/ 800m cruising in Z4, 96–104% Run FTP/ 200m quick finish
	Spin 5 min. between sets
	Cooldown: 10 min. easy run
	
	This workout replicates draft-legal racing with high-intensity bike-to-run efforts. Set up turbo trainer on track for quick transition.
		SWIM
		
		Aerobic Endurance Drills // **1500**
		
		Warm-up: 500 choice
		Main set:
		8 × 50 drills for technique limiter, 20 sec. rest
		6 × 50 fast with good form, 30 sec. rest
		Cooldown: 300 easy

Sun.	**RUN** **Aerobic Base Building** // **1 hr.** 60 min. Z1/Z2, 65–88% Run FTP *Light and easy with good form. Cadence at 90+ spm.*	**SWIM** **Muscular Endurance** // **2700** **Warm-up:** 400 choice, 1 min. rest; 4 × 50 descend, 15 sec. rest **Main set:** 300 swim, 10 sec. rest 3 × 100 at 100 threshold — 5 sec., 10 sec. rest 300 pull, 20 sec. rest; 2 × 150 as 100 swim/ 50 kick, 30 sec. rest 300 swim, 10 sec. rest 3 × 100 at 100 threshold — 5 sec., 10 sec. rest 4 × 25 fast, 30 sec. rest **Cooldown:** 200 easy

TOTAL » 12 HR. 5 MIN.

WEEK 14 ◢ BUILD 2

	SESSION 1	SESSION 2
Mon.	**REST DAY**	

Tues.	**RUN**
	Test Set // 50 min.
	LTHR or RTP. See pp. 235–238 for details.
		SWIM
		Aerobic Endurance // 2750
		Warm-up: 200 swim, 100 kick, 200 pull, all with 30 sec. rest
		4 × 50 drills, 15 sec. rest
		Main set:
		6 × 250, 15 sec. rest
		  200 swim at threshold — 5 sec.
		  50 steady kick
		4 × 25 fast, 20 sec. rest
		Cooldown: 200 choice

Wed.	**BIKE** **FTP Test** // 1 hr. *If you do not have a power meter, do LTHR. See pp. 234–235 for details.*	
Thurs.	**SWIM** **STP Test** // 2100 *See p. 234 for details.*	**STRENGTH** **Pure Strength 2** // 30 min. *This is the last strength training session of the program. See p. 252 for exercises.*

	SESSION 1	SESSION 2
Fri.	**BIKE** **Aerobic Recovery // 30 min.** 30 min. Z1, <56% FTP *Focus on smooth, even pedal stroke.*	**RUN** **Aerobic Recovery // 20 min.** 20 min. Z1, <75% Run FTP *Controlled and relaxed.*
Sat.	**RUN** **Aerobic Rolling Course // 1 hr.** 1 hr. Z1–Z3, 65–95% Run FTP *Focus on proud, upright form. Allow heart rate to gradually rise to Z3, but don't force it up.*	**SWIM** **Aerobic Endurance Form Work // 1900** **Warm-up:** 300 choice, a mix of swim, pull, and kick **Main set:** 6 × 100 easy, 30 sec. rest 4 × 200, 30 sec. rest **Cooldown:** 200 easy *Focus on form. Aim for 55–70 strokes/min.*
Sun.	**BIKE** **Endurance Recovery // 1 hr. 20 min.** 80 min. Z1/Z2, 45–75% FTP *Don't exceed Z2 for more than a few seconds at a time as when accelerating from a stop or going up a short hill. Comfortably high rpm.*	

FINAL REST AND TEST WEEK. GETTING SOME LAST FITNESS
NUMBERS NAILED DOWN AND PREPARING THE BODY FOR
THE FINAL PEAK PHASE OF TRAINING.

TOTAL » 8 HR. 20 MIN.

LEVEL 2

	SESSION 1	SESSION 2
Mon.	**REST DAY**	

Tues.

SESSION 1

RUN

Anaerobic Speed // 40 min.

Warm-up: 15 min. with 8 strides
Main set:
6 sets:
   300m, 45 sec. rest
   200m build to Z5a/Z5b, 105–124% Run FTP,
   2 min. rest
Cooldown: 5 min.

*Focus on controlled speed. Get into Z5a,
especially by the end of the 200 in each set.
Follow recovery times closely—this is very
important! Smooth but fast!*

SESSION 2

SWIM

Speed // 2400

Warm-up: 200 swim, 100 kick, 200 pull,
all with 30 sec. rest
4 × 50 drill, 15 sec. rest; 4 × 50 descend,
15 sec. rest
Main set:
100 very easy swim between sets:
2 × 200 fast, 90 sec. rest
4 × 100 fast, 90 sec. rest
4 × 50 fast, 1 min. rest
4 × 25 fast, 1 min. rest
Cooldown: 100 easy

Wed.

BRICK

Anaerobic Capacity + Tempo Run // 1 hr. 15 min.

Warm-up: 20 min. ride
Main set:
5 × 3 min. on/3 min. off
Cooldown: 10 min. spin
Run off the bike: 15 min.

*3-min. bike intervals should be just faster than
race pace Z4/Z5a, 91–120% FTP, spinning in Z1,
when "off." For the run, build to Z3, 89–95%
Run FTP, and hold steady.*

Thurs.

SWIM

Tri-Specific // 2750

Warm-up: 200 choice, 30 sec. rest;
9 × 50 as 3 × stroke/drill/fast, 15 sec. rest
Main set:
8 × 25 fast, 30 sec. rest
4 × 200 race pace, 20 sec. rest
100 easy, 30 sec. rest
4 × 75 fast, 30 sec. rest
500 as 100 build/400 race pace
4 × 25 very fast, 30 sec. rest
Cooldown: 100 swim

	SESSION 1	SESSION 2
Fri.	**RUN** **Neuromuscular // 30 min.** **Warm-up:** 20 min. Z1/Z2, 65–88% Run FTP **Main set:** 6 × 30 strides, >105% Run FTP, with walking recoveries **Cooldown:** 5 min. *Strides are best done on grass or soft surface. Aim for 19–20 sec. Fast but controlled.*	**BIKE** **Aerobic Recovery // 35 min.** 35 min. Z1, <56% FTP *Focus on smooth, even pedal stroke.*

Sat.	**RUN**
	Aerobic Base Building // 45 min.
	45 min. Z1/Z2, 65–88% Run FTP
	Light and easy with good form. Cadence at 90+ spm.
		SWIM
		Speed // 1500
		Warm-up: 400 choice, 30 sec. rest; 4 × 50 drill, 15 sec. rest; 4 × 50 descend, 15 sec. rest
		Main set:
		4 sets:
		    25 as 12.5 easy/12.5 fast, 30 sec. rest
		    25 as 12.5 fast/12.5 easy, 30 sec. rest
		    25 fast, 30 sec. rest; 25 easy, 30 sec. rest
		    25 very fast, 30 sec. rest
		Rest 2 min. between sets
		Cooldown: 200 easy

Sun.	**BRICK**
	**Bike Intervals + 1600m Run //
	1 hr. 35 min.**
	Warm-up: 20 min. ride
	Main set:
	3 sets:
	    5 min. of 15 sec. on/15 sec. off spin
	    800m run, 5 min. jog
	    800m run, 5 min. spin
	Cooldown: 10 min. jog
	Bike "on" intervals are Z5a, >106% FTP. Run immediately after, faster than race pace in high Z4/low Z5a, 100–110% Run FTP. Back off the pace to Z3, <95% Run FTP, for 5 min., then hit it again for the next 800m.
		SWIM
		Aerobic Endurance Drills // 1400
		Warm-up: 400 choice
		Main set:
		8 × 50 drills for technique limiter, 20 sec. rest
		6 × 50 fast with good form, 30 sec. rest
		Cooldown: 300 easy

NO MORE STRENGTH TRAINING. TIME TO GET SHARP AND READY TO RACE!

TOTAL » 8 HR. 40 MIN.

LEVEL 2

	SESSION 1	SESSION 2
Mon.	**REST DAY**	

Tues.

RUN	SWIM
Neuromuscular // 40 min.	**Speed // 1800**
Warm-up: 20 min. **Main set:** 6 × 1 min. accelerations, 2 min. recovery **Cooldown:** 5 min. *Z1 and Z2, <88% Run FTP, for most of run.* *1 min. efforts are at race pace.*	**Warm-up:** 200 choice, 30 sec. rest 4 × 50 drill, 15 sec. rest; 4 × 50 descend, 15 sec. rest **Main set:** 100 easy swim between sets: 8 × 25 as odds fast/evens easy, 30 sec. rest 4 × 50 as 25 all-out/25 easy, 30 sec. rest 4 × 50 very fast, 1 min. rest 4 × 25 very fast, 1 min. rest **Cooldown:** 200 very easy

Wed.

BRICK	
Bike Neuromuscular Power + **Aerobic Run // 1 hr. 15 min.**	
Warm-up: 25 min. ride **Main set:** 6 × 90 sec. accelerations on the bike, 3 min. recovery Spin 8 min. between sets **Run off the bike:** 15 min. *Build to Z5a, >106% FTP, in the bike accelerations.* *For the run, just find your legs and hold steady.*	

Thurs.

SWIM	
Speed // 1900	
Warm-up: 300 choice **Main set:** 4 sets: 4 × 75 as 25 fast/25 slow/25 fast, 10 sec. rest Rest 1 min. between sets 8 × 25 fast, 30 sec. rest **Cooldown:** 200 easy	

	SESSION 1	SESSION 2
Fri.	**BRICK** **Bike Neuromuscular Power + Aerobic Run** // 55 min. **Main set:** 45 min. ride with 5 sec. jump once every 5 min. **Run off the bike:** 10 min. *Ride is mostly easy in Z1 and Z2, <75% FTP. Eight jumps in total, going over Z5a, >106% FTP, each time. For the run, just find your legs and hold steady.*	
Sat.	**SWIM** **Aerobic Endurance** // 600 *Check out the race swim venue if possible. Do 8 very short accelerations (25–50m) at race pace. Easy swimming between each for 30 sec. Be sure to check out the start and finish area. This is best done in the morning near race time.*	**BRICK** **Bike Accelerations + Run Acceleration** // 35 min. 20 min. ride 15 min. run *Do this on the race course, if possible. Include 3–4 short, race pace efforts. Note landmarks. Afterward, tighten all bolts on your bike.*
Sun.	**RACE DAY!**	*You've put in some great work and have prepared properly. Now, get out, execute your race plan, and have fun!*

TOTAL » **5 HR. 15 MIN. + RACE**

9

THE LEVEL 3 PROGRAM

The Level 3 Program is certainly aimed at athletes who are fast. If you're near the podium in your age group, then the Level 3 Program will help you get to the top step and onward to a national level of competition. While you may not be a professional-level triathlete, you can take confidence from knowing that this is the type of plan a pro or aspiring pro would use.

But if you are a seasoned triathlete who sits closer to the middle or back of the pack and are seriously seeking to improve that position, then this plan is for you too. Committing to it will help you improve your own personal best—whatever it may be—and chase those faster times.

In sum, the Level 3 Program is for any triathlete who wants to see how far he or she can push short-course racing. With a focus on competing at your best, this plan will require more time, more energy, and more commitment to doing the extras that help you stay healthy and able to perform on those big workout days.

The plan's 16-week progression will take you from little training (but with a strong, previously established background in triathlon) to race day. The race you're planning for should be the race you want to shine at, but bear in mind that unlike in long-course racing, it won't be the only race at which you can do well.

If you are planning to follow the Level 3 schedule, then you've made the decision to go faster, which demands a conscious mindset shift. How you approach the next 16 weeks will make all the difference.

1. **FOLLOW THE PLAN.** Athletes with a less competitive goal in mind have a lot more leeway when it comes to training. If you're interested in going faster than you have in the past, it's important to follow a plan and stick to the workouts prescribed. A bike ride is never just a bike ride—advanced triathletes need to follow the structure of the ride for that day in order to improve.

2. **BE CONSISTENT.** While beginners can be more relaxed about taking extra easy days or not sticking precisely to a plan, advanced athletes should do the training as written. The Level 3 Program is precisely crafted—everything is meant to be done, and in the order prescribed.

GAUGE YOUR EFFORT

In the advanced plan that follows, you'll see both heart-rate zones and power zones in many of the workouts. We strongly suggest that Level 3 triathletes invest in a cycling power meter to take full advantage of precise training zones in each workout to get the most objective sense of effort. A running power meter is also important if many of your workouts will be performed on hilly or rough terrain to give you an accurate measure of output. Either way, be sure to perform all of the benchmark tests throughout the program to reestablish your zones periodically.

3. **EFFORT MATTERS.** Go hard when it's time to go hard, and go easy when it's time to go easy. Remember, you need to perform your best on hard days, and you can't do that if you're not recovering on easy days. Races can't be won on rest and recovery days, but they can definitely be lost there if improperly executed. It's crucial to take recovery seriously in order to get "up" for the next tough workout.

4. **PREPARE TO PUSH.** This plan is for athletes looking to get faster. This means more volume, more intensity, and more specificity than the Level 1 and Level 2 Programs. You'll need to push yourself closer to your limits to improve. Get comfortable with the uncomfortable.

5. **SPECIFICITY COUNTS.** While many of the principles in short-course training can make an athlete faster at longer events, the Level 3 Program uses specificity that requires shorter, more intense efforts. If it's any consolation, it may hurt more, but for less time. Furthermore, the intensity comes earlier in the short-course plan than you may have experienced in a long-course plan. Prepare yourself for that.

6. **THE SWIM CARRIES A LOT OF WEIGHT.** In short-course racing, swimming plays a major role, so it's important to spend more time training for the swim. If draft-legal racing is on your radar, improving your swim is crucial because it allows you to be in a faster bike pack near the front of the race. Get left behind in T1 of a draft-legal race and you'll have a long, hard day ahead of you.

WEEK 1 ◢ PREP 1

PHASE
1

LEVEL 3

	SESSION 1	SESSION 2
Mon.	**STRENGTH** **Anatomical Adaptation** // 1 hr. *See p. 252 for exercises.*	
Tues.	**RUN** **Aerobic Base Building** // 40 min. 40 min. Z1/Z2, 65–88% Run FTP *Light and easy with good form.* *Cadence at 90+ spm.*	**SWIM** **Aerobic Endurance Form Work** // 3300 **Warm-up:** 300 swim, 100 kick, 300 pull **Main set:** 5 × 200 easy, 30 sec. rest 4 × 300 easy, 30 sec. rest **Cooldown:** 8 × 50, 20 sec. rest *Focus on form. Aim for 55–70 strokes/min.*
Wed.	**BIKE** **Endurance Base Building** // 1 hr. 15 min. 75 min. Z1/Z2, 45–75% FTP *Keep cadence high.*	
Thurs.	**SWIM** **Aerobic Endurance Intervals** // 2550 **Warm-up:** 100 easy swim, 50 easy kick, 100 moderate swim, 50 moderate kick, 100 swim build speed, 50 kick build speed, all with 15 sec. rest **Main set:** 4 × 300 moderate, 10 sec. rest Rest 2 min. between sets 300 kick, steady 6 × 50 relaxed speed, 15 sec. rest **Cooldown:** 300 easy *Decrease times with each work interval* *for the first set.*	**STRENGTH** **Anatomical Adaptation** // 1 hr. *See p. 252 for exercises.*

SESSION 1	SESSION 2
Fri. **RUN** **Aerobic Recovery** // **30 min.** 30 min. Z1, <75% Run FTP *Controlled and relaxed.*	**BIKE** **Aerobic Recovery** // **40 min.** 40 min. Z1, <56% FTP *Focus on smooth, even pedal stroke.*
Sat. **SWIM** **Aerobic Endurance Drills** // **2000** **Warm-up:** 800 choice **Main set:** 8 × 50 drills for technique limiter, 20 sec. rest 6 × 50 fast with good form, 30 sec. rest **Cooldown:** 500 easy	**RUN** **Aerobic Moderate Mid-Distance** // **1 hr.** 60 min. Z1–Z3, 65–95% Run FTP *Mostly Z1/Z2, <88% Run FTP. Flat to rolling terrain. Aerobic work with good form.*
Sun. **BIKE** **Endurance Pure Base** // **1 hr. 30 min.** 90 min. Z1–Z3, 45–80% FTP *It's okay to spike the power a bit into Z3 on hills or into headwinds. Mostly smooth and steady, pure base building.*	

HERE WE GO! THIS PHASE IS DESIGNED TO GET YOU UP AND RUNNING. FIRST, A BUILD WEEK, THEN NEXT WEEK IS YOUR FIRST ROUND OF BASELINE TESTS.

TOTAL » 10 HR. 10 MIN.

PHASE 1

	SESSION 1	SESSION 2
Mon.	**STRENGTH** **Anatomical Adaptation // 1 hr.** *See p. 252 for exercises.*	
Tues.	**RUN** **Test Set // 50 min.** *LTHR or RTP. See pp. 235–238 for details.*	**SWIM** **Aerobic Endurance // 3000** **Warm-up:** 200 swim, 100 kick, 200 pull, all with 30 sec. rest 8 × 50 drill, 15 sec. rest **Main set:** Rest 1 min. between sets: 8 × 150 easier than threshold, 10 sec. rest 6 × 75 easier than threshold, 10 sec. rest 4 × 25 fast, 30 sec. rest 150 kick **Cooldown:** 200 swim
Wed.	**BIKE** **FTP Test // 1 hr.** *If you do not have a power meter, do LTHR. See pp. 234–235 for details.*	
Thurs.	**SWIM** **STP Test // 2100** *See p. 234 for details.*	**STRENGTH** **Anatomical Adaptation // 1 hr.** *See p. 252 for exercises.*

LEVEL 3

	SESSION 1	SESSION 2
Fri.	**RUN** **Aerobic Recovery // 30 min.** 30 min. Z1, <75% Run FTP *Controlled and relaxed.*	**BIKE** **Aerobic Recovery // 45 min.** 45 min. easy spin Z1, <56% FTP *Focus on a smooth, even pedal stroke.*
Sat.	**RUN** **Aerobic Moderate Mid-Distance // 1 hr. 10 min.** 70 min. Z1–Z3, 65–95% Run FTP *Mostly Z1/Z2, <88% Run FTP. Flat to rolling terrain. Aerobic work with good form.*	**SWIM** **Aerobic Endurance Form Work // 2900** **Warm-up:** 100 swim, 100 kick, 100 pull, all with 30 sec. rest **Main set:** Easy effort: 5 × 200, 30 sec. rest 4 × 300, 30 sec. rest **Cooldown:** 400 easy *Focus on form. Aim for 55–70 strokes/min.*
Sun.	**BIKE** **Endurance Pure Base // 1 hr. 45 min.** 105 min. Z1–Z3, 45–80% FTP *It's okay to spike the power a bit into Z3 on hills or into headwinds. Mostly smooth and steady, pure base building.*	

TOTAL » 10 HR. 40 MIN.

WEEK 3 ◢ BASE 1

	SESSION 1	SESSION 2
Mon.	**STRENGTH** **Fitness Strength** // 1 hr. *See p. 252 for exercises.*	
Tues.	**SWIM** **Aerobic Endurance** // 3000 **Warm-up:** 200 swim, 100 kick, 200 pull, all with 30 sec. rest 8 × 50 drill, 15 sec. rest **Main set:** 2 sets: 3 × 200 at threshold + 10 sec., 15 sec. rest 200 kick or IM, 2 min. rest (butterfly, backstroke, breaststroke, freestyle) 300 pull **Cooldown:** 200 choice	**RUN** **Neuromuscular** // 50 min. **Warm-up:** 40 min. Z1/Z2, 65–88% Run FTP **Main set:** 6 × 30 strides, <105% Run FTP, with walking recoveries **Cooldown:** 5 min. *Strides are best done on grass or soft surface. Aim for 19–20 sec. Fast but controlled.*
Wed.	**BRICK** **Bike Endurance Progression + Aerobic Run** // 1 hr. 40 min. **Main set:** 80 min. ride **Run off the bike:** 20 min. Z1/Z2, <88% Run FTP *First part of ride should be in Z1/Z2, 45–75% FTP. Average in Z2/Z3, 56–90% FTP, at halfway point; avoid Z4. For the run, just find your legs and hold steady.*	
Thurs.	**SWIM** **Muscular Endurance** // 3200 **Warm-up:** 200 choice, 30 sec. rest 5 × 100 descend 1–5 (each set faster than previous), 30 sec. rest **Main set:** 1000 steady, 30 sec. rest 500 as 75 easy/25 fast, 1 min. rest 8 × 100 race pace, 15 sec. rest **Cooldown:** 200 easy	**STRENGTH** **Fitness Strength** // 1 hr. *See p. 252 for exercises.*

	SESSION 1	SESSION 2
Fri.	**RUN** **Aerobic Recovery // 35 min.** 35 min. Z1, <75% Run FTP *Controlled and relaxed.*	**BIKE** **Endurance Base Building // 50 min.** 50 min. Z1/Z2, 45–75% FTP *Keep cadence high.*
Sat.	**RUN** **Aerobic Rolling Course // 1 hr. 20 min.** 80 min. Z1–Z3, 65–95% Run FTP *Focus on proud, upright form. Allow heart rate to gradually rise to Z3, but don't force it up.*	**SWIM** **Aerobic Endurance Drills // 2000** **Warm-up:** 800 choice of free, stroke, pull, and kick **Main set:** 8 × 50 drills for technique limiter, 20 sec. rest 6 × 50 fast with good form, 30 sec. rest **Cooldown:** 500 easy
Sun.	**BIKE** **Endurance Cadence Drills // 2 hr.** **Warm-up:** 1 hr. **Main set:** 6 × 1 min. on/1 min. off 10 min. spin 2 × 5 min. on/5 min. off 2 × 1 min. on/1 min. off **Cooldown:** 14 min. *1 min. intervals: Z3/Z4, 76–105% FTP.* *5 min. intervals: 100 rpm Z3, 76–90% FTP.* *Spin in Z1, <56% FTP, for "off" intervals.*	

STARTING TO BUILD SOME GOOD BASE!

TOTAL » 12 HR.

	SESSION 1	SESSION 2
Mon.	**STRENGTH** **Fitness Strength** // 1 hr. *See p. 252 for exercises.*	

Tues.	**RUN**
	Neuromuscular // 1 hr.
	Warm-up: 45 min. Z1–Z3, 65–95% Run FTP
	Main set:
	6 × 200m strides, <105% Run FTP, with 200m jog recoveries
	Cooldown: 5 min.
	Build from slow to fast with each stride set.
		SWIM
		Aerobic Endurance // 3400
		Warm-up: 300 swim, 200 kick, 200 pull, all with 30 sec. rest
		8 × 50 drill or stroke (no free), 15 sec. rest
		Main set:
		3 sets:
		   500 free at 100 threshold pace + 5 sec., 20 sec. rest
		   200 kick, 30 sec. rest
		Cooldown: 200 easy

Wed.	**BRICK** **Tempo Bike + Aerobic Run** // 1 hr. 50 min. **Warm-up:** 30 min. ride **Main set:** 45 min. Z3, 76–90% FTP **Cooldown:** 15 min. spin **Run off the bike:** 20 min. Z1/Z2, 65–88% Run FTP *For the run, just find your legs and hold steady.*	

Thurs.	**SWIM**
	Muscular Endurance // 3300
	Warm-up: 200 swim, 100 kick, 200 pull, all with 30 sec. rest
	8 × 50 drill, 15 sec. rest
	Main set:
	Swims at 100 threshold pace + 5 sec.
	   500 free, 400 pull, each with 20 sec. rest
	   300 free, 200 IM, each with 15 sec. rest
	100 free fast, 1 min. rest
	5 × 100 at threshold, 10 sec. rest; 200 kick
	Cooldown: 200 swim
		STRENGTH
		Fitness Strength // 1 hr.
		See p. 252 for exercises.

	SESSION 1	SESSION 2
Fri.	**RUN** **Aerobic Base Building** // 35 min. 35 min. Z1/Z2, 65–88% Run FTP *Light and easy with good form.* *Cadence at 90+ spm.*	**BIKE** **Endurance Base Building** // 1 hr. 1 hr. Z1/Z2, 45–75% FTP *Keep cadence high.*
Sat.	**RUN** **Aerobic Rolling Course** // 1 hr. 30 min. 90 min. Z1–Z3, 65–95% Run FTP *Focus on proud, upright form. Allow heart rate to gradually rise to Z3, but don't force it up.*	**SWIM** **Aerobic Endurance Drills** // 2000 **Warm-up:** 800 choice **Main set:** 8 × 50 drills for technique limiter, 20 sec. rest 6 × 50 fast with good form, 30 sec. rest **Cooldown:** 500 easy
Sun.	**BRICK** **Endurance Bike + Aerobic Run** // **2 hr. 40 min.** **Warm-up:** 30 min. ride **Main set:** 90 min. Z2/Z3, 56–90% FTP, with 8 sec. bursts to Z7, >150% FTP, every 10 min. **Cooldown:** 15 min. spin **Run off the bike:** 25 min. Z1/Z2, 65–88% Run FTP *Relatively high cadence for the bike warm-up (90 rpm). Bursts should be 80% of a full sprint, 105+ rpm. For the run, just find your legs and hold steady.*	

TOTAL » 13 HR. 30 MIN.

PHASE 2

LEVEL 3

	SESSION 1	SESSION 2
Mon.	**REST DAY**	

Tues.	**SWIM**
	 Aerobic Endurance // 3000
	 Warm-up: 200 swim, 100 kick, 200 pull, all with 30 sec. rest
	 8 × 50 drill, 15 sec. rest
	 Main set:
	 3 sets:
	     300 swim at threshold + 5 sec., 15 sec. rest
	     200 steady swim at threshold + 5 sec., 15 sec. rest
	     100 fast, 1 min. rest
	 100 kick
	 Cooldown: 200 swim
		RUN
		 Aerobic Moderate Mid-Distance // 50 min.
		 50 min. Z1–Z3, 65–95% Run FTP
		 Mostly Z1/Z2, <75% Run FTP. Flat to rolling terrain. Aerobic work with good form.

Wed.	**BIKE** **Neuromuscular Power // 1 hr.** **Warm-up:** 30 min. Z1/Z2, 45–75% FTP **Main set:** 8 spin-ups, 2 min. recovery **Cooldown:** 10 min. spin *When you start to bounce in the saddle, back off and recover. Don't push a big gear. Keep your legs sharp and increase cadence, not power.*	
Thurs.	**SWIM** **Muscular Endurance // 3000** **Warm-up:** 200 swim, 100 kick, 200 pull, all with 30 sec. rest 4 × 50 drill, 15 sec. rest **Main set:** 4 × 250 as 100 moderate/50 build/ 100 moderate, 20 sec. rest 1 min. rest 2 × 500 with second 250 10 sec. faster than first, 30 sec. rest 1 min. rest **Cooldown:** 300 swim	**STRENGTH** **Fitness Strength // 1 hr.** *See p. 252 for exercises.*

	SESSION 1	SESSION 2
Fri.	**RUN** **Aerobic Recovery** // **30 min.** 30 min. Z1, <75% Run FTP *Controlled and relaxed.*	**BIKE** **Aerobic Recovery** // **40 min.** 40 min. Z1, <56% FTP *Focus on smooth, even pedal stroke.*
Sat.	**RUN** **Aerobic Long Run** // **1 hr. 15 min.** 75 min. *Get at least half of the time in Z2, 76–88% Run FTP. Focus on good form and quick cadence.*	**SWIM** **Aerobic Endurance Form Work** // **3200** **Warm-up:** 500 choice 6 × 50 drill, 15 sec. rest. **Main set:** Easy effort: 5 × 200, 30 sec. rest 4 × 300, 30 sec. rest **Cooldown:** 100 kick, 100 swim *Focus on form. Aim for 55–70 strokes/min.*
Sun.	**BIKE** **Endurance Recovery** // **1 hr. 30 min.** 90 min. Z1/Z2, <75% FTP *Don't exceed Z2 for more than a few seconds at a time as when accelerating from a stop or going up a short hill. Comfortably high rpm.*	

LIGHTER THIS WEEK. LET THE BODY AND MIND RECOVER
FROM THE LAST TWO WEEKS OF SOLID BASE BUILDING.

TOTAL » **9 HR. 50 MIN.**

LEVEL 3

	SESSION 1	SESSION 2
Mon.	**STRENGTH** **Fitness Strength** // 1 hr. *See p. 252 for exercises.*	
Tues.	**RUN** **Tempo** // 1 hr. **Warm-up:** 20 min. Z1/Z2, 65–88% Run FTP **Main set:** 20 min. Z2/Z3, 76–95% Run FTP 20 min. steady Z3, 89–95% Run FTP *Pace and heart rate should progressively increase as the run progresses.*	**SWIM** **Muscular Endurance** // 3300 **Warm-up:** 400 swim, 200 kick, 200 pull, all with 30 sec. rest; 8 × 50 drill, 15 sec. rest **Main set:** 300 swim, 300 pull, each with 15 sec. rest 100 fast swim, 1 min. rest 200 swim, 200 pull, each with 15 sec. rest 100 fast swim, 1 min. rest 100 swim, 100 pull, each with 15 sec. rest 100 fast swim, 1 min. rest; 3 × 100 kick, 15 sec. rest **Cooldown:** 300 choice
Wed.	**BRICK** **Bike Power Development + Aerobic Run** // 1 hr. 50 min. **Warm-up:** 20 min. ride **Main set:** 3 min. at 40 rpm, 2 min. recovery 6 min. at 50 rpm, 3 min. recovery 2 × 12 min. at 60 rpm, 4 min. recovery 6 min. at 50 rpm, 3 min. recovery 3 min. at 40 rpm, 2 min. recovery **Cooldown:** 10 min. very easy spin **Run off the bike:** 20 min. Z1/Z2, 88% Run FTP *Bike recoveries should all be in Z1, <56% FTP, at a cadence of 80–100 rpm. Intervals should go from low Z4, <95% FTP, in the shortest sets to Z3, <90% FTP, in the longest. For the run, just find your legs and hold steady.*	
Thurs.	**SWIM** **Threshold** // 3500 **Warm-up:** 200 swim, 100 kick, 200 pull, all with 30 sec. rest 8 × 50 drill, 15 sec. rest **Main set:** Rest 30 sec. between sets: 3 × 350 swim/pull/swim at threshold, 15 sec. rest 3 × 250 swim/pull/swim at threshold, 15 sec. rest 3 × 150 swim/pull/swim at threshold, 15 sec. rest 3 × 50 swim/pull/swim at threshold, 20 sec. rest **Cooldown:** 200 swim	**STRENGTH** **Fitness Strength** // 1 hr. *See p. 252 for exercises.*

	SESSION 1	SESSION 2
Fri.	**RUN** **Neuromuscular** // 30 min. **Warm-up:** 20 min. Z1/Z2, 65–88% Run FTP **Main set:** 6 × 30 strides, >105% Run FTP, with walking recoveries **Cooldown:** 5 min. *Strides are best done on grass or soft surface. Aim for 19–20 sec. Fast but controlled.*	**BIKE** **Endurance Base Building** // 1 hr. 60 min. Z1/Z2, 45–75% FTP *Keep cadence high.*

Sat.	**RUN**
	
	Long Run // 1 hr. 30 min.
	
	90 min.
	The first 50 min. of the run are all aerobic in Z1 and Z2, <88% Run FTP. Tempo finish, last 40 min. in Z3, 89–95% Run FTP. Relax! Record your tempo pace during the last 30 min.
		SWIM
		
		Muscular Endurance // 3000
		
		Warm-up: 200 swim, 200 stroke, 200 kick, all with 30 sec. rest
		4 × 50 drill or stroke, 15 sec. rest
		Main set:
		Swims at 100 threshold + 5 sec. with 20 sec. rest post kick or pull:
		  100 swim, 50 kick; 200 swim, 50 kick
		  300 swim, 50 kick; 500 pull
		  300 swim, 50 kick; 200 swim, 50 kick
		  100 swim, 50 kick
		Cooldown: 200 easy

Sun.	**BRICK** **Bike Endurance Intervals + Aerobic Run** // 2 hr. 50 min. **Warm-up:** 45 min. ride **Main set:** 5 × 1 min. primer repeats, 2 min. recovery 4 × 15 min. repeats, 5 min. recovery **Cooldown:** 15 min. spin **Run off the bike:** 15 min. Z1/Z2, 65–88% Run FTP *Primer repeats in Z3/Z4, 76–105% FTP. 15 min. repeats in Z3, 76–90% FTP. This should feel smooth and steady. Lock in the pace and hold. For the run, just find your legs and hold steady.*	**SWIM** **Aerobic Endurance Drills** // 1500 **Warm-up:** 500 choice **Main set:** 8 × 50 drills for technique limiter, 20 sec. rest 6 × 50 fast with good form, 30 sec. rest **Cooldown:** 300 easy

GETTING IN SOME MORE BASE WORK. VOLUME WILL CONTINUE TO INCREASE, AND INTENSITY WILL RISE JUST A BIT TOO. THERE'S ALSO AN ADDED SWIM EACH WEEK.

TOTAL » 14 HR. 25 MIN.

	SESSION 1	SESSION 2
Mon.	**STRENGTH** **Fitness Strength** // 1 hr. *See p. 252 for exercises.*	
Tues.	**RUN** **Speed Strength** // 1 hr. 10 min. **Warm-up:** 35 min. moderate **Main set:** 10 × 80m hill sprints Jog downhill for recovery 2 miles Z4+ **Cooldown:** 5 min. jog *Do the hill sprints on a 6–10% grade.* *Fast and powerful. 2-mile run is at tempo pace.*	**SWIM** **Muscular Endurance** // 3400 **Warm-up:** 300 swim, 100 kick, 200 pull, all with 30 sec. rest 8 × 50 drill or stroke (no free), 15 sec. rest **Main set:** 3 × 300 steady pull, 15 sec. rest 6 × 150 threshold swim, 10 sec. rest 6 × 50 speed swim, 30 sec. rest 100 easy kick **Cooldown:** 200 choice
Wed.	**BRICK** **Bike Power Development +** **Aerobic Run** // 1 hr. 55 min. **Warm-up:** 20 min. ride **Main set:** 6 × 5 min. at 55 rpm Z4, 91–105% FTP, 5 min. recovery **Cooldown:** 20 min. spin **Run off the bike:** 15 min. Z1/Z2, 65–88% Run FTP *Do bike intervals on flat or slightly uphill terrain.* *Constant pressure on the pedals. For the run,* *just find your legs and hold steady.*	

Thurs.	**SWIM**
	
	Threshold // 3500
	
	Warm-up: 300 swim, 200 kick, 200 pull,
	all with 30 sec. rest
	8 × 50 drill or stroke (no free), 15 sec. rest
	Main set:
	2 sets:
	   300 steady pull, 20 sec. rest
	   6 × 100 at threshold, 10 sec. rest
	300 pull
	1 min. rest
	100 easy kick
	Cooldown: 200 easy
		STRENGTH
		
		Fitness Strength // 1 hr.
		
		See p. 252 for exercises.

LEVEL 3

SESSION 1	SESSION 2
Fri. **RUN** **Neuromuscular // 30 min.** **Warm-up:** 20 min. Z1/Z2, 65–88% Run FTP **Main set:** 6 × 30 strides, >105% Run FTP, with walking recoveries **Cooldown:** 5 min. *Strides are best done on grass or soft surface. Aim for 19–20 sec. Fast but controlled.*	**BIKE** **Endurance Base Building // 1 hr.** 60 min. Z1/Z2, 45–75% FTP *Keep cadence high.*
Sat. **RUN** **Long Run // 1 hr. 40 min.** **Warm-up:** 20 min. **Main set:** 70 min. Z3, 89–95% Run FTP **Cooldown:** 10 min. *Focus on good form with 90+ spm cadence.*	**SWIM** **Aerobic Endurance // 3300** **Warm-up:** 400 swim, 300 pull, each with 30 sec. rest 8 × 50 drill, 15 sec. rest **Main set:** Swims at threshold + 5 sec. per 100 4 × 200, 15 sec. rest 4 × 150, 15 sec. rest 4 × 100, 15 sec. rest 4 × 50 fast, 30 sec. rest **Cooldown:** 200 choice
Sun. **BRICK** **Endurance Bike + Aerobic Run // 3 hr. 20 min.** **Main set:** 3 hr. ride Z1/Z2, 45–75% FTP **Run off the bike:** 20 min. *Ride should mostly be in Z1/Z2. Okay to spike into Z3, <90% FTP, every once in a while. Plan accordingly with nutrition and hydration.*	**SWIM** **Aerobic Endurance Drills // 1800** **Warm-up:** 800 choice **Main set:** 8 × 50 drills for technique limiter, 20 sec. rest 6 × 50 fast with good form, 30 sec. rest **Cooldown:** 300 easy

TOTAL » 15 HR. 35 MIN.

WEEK 8 ◢ BASE 2

	SESSION 1	SESSION 2
Mon.	**REST DAY**	
Tues.	**RUN** **Test Set // 50 min.** *LTHR or RTP. See pp. 235–238 for details.*	**SWIM** **Muscular Endurance // 2400** **Warm-up:** 200 swim, 100 kick, 200 pull, all with 30 sec. rest; 4 × 50 drill, 15 sec. rest **Main set:** 300 swim, 300 pull, each with 15 sec. rest 100 fast swim, 1 min. rest 200 swim, 200 pull, each with 15 sec. rest 100 fast swim, 1 min. rest 100 swim, 100 pull, each 15 sec. rest 100 fast swim **Cooldown:** 200 choice
Wed.	**BIKE** **FTP Test // 1 hr.** *If you do not have a power meter, do LTHR. See pp. 234–235 for details.*	
Thurs.	**SWIM** **STP Test // 2100** *See p. 234 for details.*	**STRENGTH** **Fitness Strength // 1 hr.** *See p. 252 for exercises.*

	SESSION 1	SESSION 2
Fri.	**RUN** **Aerobic Recovery // 20 min.** 20 min. Z1, <75% Run FTP *Controlled and relaxed.*	**BIKE** **Aerobic Recovery // 30 min.** 30 min. Z1, <56% FTP *Focus on smooth, even pedal stroke.*
Sat.	**RUN** **Aerobic Long Run // 1 hr. 10 min.** 70 min. *Get at least half of the time in Z2, 76–88% Run FTP.* *Focus on good form and quick cadence.*	**SWIM** **Aerobic Endurance Form Work // 1800** **Warm-up:** 300 choice **Main set:** Easy effort: 6 × 100, 30 sec. rest 4 × 200, 30 sec. rest **Cooldown:** 100 easy *Focus on form. Aim for 55–70 strokes/min.*
Sun.	**BIKE** **Endurance Recovery // 1 hr. 30 min.** 90 min. Z1/Z2, <75% FTP *Don't exceed Z2 for more than a few seconds* *at a time as when accelerating from a stop* *or going up a short hill. Comfortably high rpm.*	

BACKING OFF THE TRAINING A BIT AND GETTING IN SOME
CHECK–IN TESTS. AFTER EACH TEST, YOU'LL NEED TO MODIFY
YOUR TRAINING ZONES.

TOTAL » 8 HR. 30 MIN.

LEVEL 3

	SESSION 1	SESSION 2
Mon.	**STRENGTH** **Pure Strength 1 // 45 min.** *See p. 252 for exercises.*	
Tues.	**SWIM** **Muscular Endurance // 3300** **Warm-up:** 200 swim, 100 kick, 200 pull, all with 30 sec. rest 6 × 50 drill, 15 sec. rest **Main set:** 100 IM, 200 swim, each with 15 sec. rest 400 pull, 600 swim, 400 pull, all with 20 sec. rest 200 swim, 15 sec. rest 100 IM, 1 min. rest 6 × 50 fast, 30 sec. rest **Cooldown:** 200 easy	**RUN** **Speed Strength // 1 hr. 5 min.** **Warm-up:** 15 min. **Main set:** 6 × 800m uphill run Jog downhill between each one **Cooldown:** 10 min. easy *Hill should be 4–6% grade. Build to Z4, 96–104% Run FTP, on each set. Focus on driving the legs and arms up the hill.*
Wed.	**BRICK** **Bike Neuromuscular Power + Aerobic Run // 1 hr. 50 min.** **Warm-up:** 30 min. ride **Main set:** 3 sets: 10 min. of 15 sec. on/15 sec. off Spin 5 min. between sets **Cooldown:** 15 min. ride **Run off the bike:** 20 min. Z1/Z2, <88% Run FTP *On the bike, 15-sec. "on" intervals are >150% FTP, "off" intervals are easy spin. For the run, just find your legs and hold steady.*	

Thurs.	**SWIM**
	
	Tri-Specific // 3200
	
	Warm-up: 200 swim, 100 kick, 200 pull, all with 30 sec. rest
	6 × 50 drill or stroke (no free), 15 sec. rest
	Main set:
	2 sets:
	   200 fast, 10 sec. rest
	   300 steady swim, 15 sec. rest
	   400 pull, 30 sec. rest
	200 easy kick; 8 × 25 fast, 30 sec. rest
	Cooldown: 200 easy
		STRENGTH
		
		Pure Strength 1 // 45 min.
		
		See p. 252 for exercises.

	SESSION 1	SESSION 2
Fri.	**RUN** **Neuromuscular** // **30 min.** **Warm-up:** 20 min. Z1/Z2, 65–88% Run FTP **Main set:** 6 × 30 strides, >105% Run FTP, with walking recoveries **Cooldown:** 5 min. *Strides are best done on grass or soft surface. Aim for 19–20 sec. Fast but controlled.*	**BIKE** **Endurance Isolated-Leg Training** // **1 hr.** **Warm-up:** 20 min. **Main set:** 20 min. as 1 min. left/1 min. right Get a total of 10 min. on each leg **Cooldown:** 20 min. spin *Do this on a trainer to have non-pedaling leg on a chair. Keep comfortably high cadence. Focus on eliminating dead spot in stroke by pushing toes forward in shoes at top.*

Sat.	**RUN**
	
	Long Run // **1 hr. 30 min.**
	
	Warm-up: 30 min.
	Main set:
	5 sets:
	  1200m Z4, 96–104% Run FTP
	  400m jog
	Cooldown: Z1 jog for duration, <75% Run FTP
	
	This should be high quality. Focus on good efforts during the 1200s.
		SWIM
		
		Threshold // **2900**
		
		Warm-up: 600 choice, 1 min. rest;
		6 × 50 drills, 15 sec. rest
		Main set:
		4 × 200, 20 sec. rest
		1 min. rest
		4 × 100, 20 sec. rest
		1 min. rest
		400 steady pull
		1 min. rest
		4 × 25 fast, 30 sec. rest; 100 easy kick
		Cooldown: 200 choice

Sun.	**BRICK** **Tempo Bike + Tempo Run** // **2 hr. 35 min.** **Warm-up:** 45 min. ride **Main set:** 45 min. tempo, 76–90% FTP 10 min. Z1, <56% FTP 2 × 10 min. Z4, 91–105% FTP, 5 min. recovery **Cooldown:** 10 min. spin **Run off the bike:** 15 min. *For the run, build to Z3, 89–95% Run FTP, and hold steady.*	**SWIM** **Aerobic Endurance Drills** // **1500** **Warm-up:** 500 choice **Main set:** 8 × 50 drills for technique limiter, 20 sec. rest 6 × 50 fast with good form, 30 sec. rest **Cooldown:** 300 easy

GETTING INTO THE BUILD PHASE HERE. VOLUME WILL DROP A BIT, BUT NOT SUBSTANTIALLY. IT WILL THEN BUILD BACK UP TO MATCH THE INTENSITY.

TOTAL » 13 HR. 40 MIN.

PHASE 3

LEVEL 3

	SESSION 1	SESSION 2
Mon.	**STRENGTH** **Pure Strength 1 // 45 min.** *See p. 252 for exercises.*	
Tues.	**SWIM** **Muscular Endurance // 3400** **Warm-up:** 200 swim, 100 kick, 200 pull, all with 30 sec. rest 6 × 50 drill or stroke (no free), 15 sec. rest **Main set:** Rest 1 min. between sets: 3 × 300, 15 sec. rest 3 × 200, 15 sec. rest 3 × 100, 15 sec. rest 3 × 200 pull, focus on power, 15 sec. rest **Cooldown:** 200 easy	**RUN** **VO₂max Fartlek // 1 hr. 5 min** **Warm-up:** 20 min. easy **Main set:** 12 × 90 sec. on, low Z5a, <110% Run FTP/ 90 sec. off, Z3, 89–95% Run FTP **Cooldown:** 10 min. easy *Not too slow on the "off" intervals; this is very important.*
Wed.	**BRICK** **Bike Neuromuscular Power + Aerobic Run // 1 hr. 50 min.** **Warm-up:** 20 min. spin **Main set:** 60 min. Z3, 76–90% FTP, with 10 sec. out-of-the-saddle bursts every 5 min., >150% FTP **Cooldown:** 10 min. spin **Run off the bike:** 20 min. Z1/Z2, <88% Run FTP *Shift up to two times to build speed on bursts. Keep cadence high. For the run, just find your legs and hold steady.*	
Thurs.	**SWIM** **Tri-Specific // 3100** **Warm-up:** 500 choice, 1 min. rest 6 × 50 drill, 15 sec. rest **Main set:** 200 fast, 10 sec. rest 8 × 100 at threshold, 10 sec. rest 200 fast, 2 min. rest 3 × 300 pull, 20 sec. rest **Cooldown:** 200 easy	**STRENGTH** **Pure Strength 1 // 45 min.** *See p. 252 for exercises.*

	SESSION 1	SESSION 2
Fri.	**RUN** **Neuromuscular** // **30 min.** **Warm-up:** 20 min. Z1/Z2, 65–88% Run FTP **Main set:** 6 × 30 strides, >105% Run FTP, with walking recoveries **Cooldown:** 5 min. *Strides are best done on grass or soft surface. Aim for 19–20 sec. Fast but controlled.*	**BIKE** **Neuromuscular Power** // **1 hr.** **Warm-up:** 30 min. Z1/Z2, 45–75% FTP **Main set:** 8 spin-ups, 2 min. recovery **Cooldown:** 10 min. spin *When you start to bounce in the saddle, back off and recover. Don't push a big gear. Keep your legs sharp and increase cadence, not power.*
Sat.	**BIKE** **Lactate Threshold** // **2 hr. 40 min.** **Warm-up:** 20 min. Z1/Z2, 45–75% FTP **Main set:** 8 × 1 min. all-out, >150% FTP, 1 min. recovery 15 min. spin 3 × 10 min. Z4, 91–105% FTP, 10 min. spin recovery 30 min. tempo, Z3, 76–90% FTP **Cooldown:** Spin for the duration	**SWIM** **Threshold** // **3000** **Warm-up:** 200 swim, 100 kick, 200 pull, all with 30 sec. rest 4 × 50 drill, 15 sec. rest **Main set:** 4 × 500 at threshold pace, 45 sec. rest **Cooldown:** 100 kick, 200 swim *Perfect form on the cooldown.*
Sun.	**BRICK** **Tempo Bike + Long Run** // **2 hr. 30 min.** **Bike set:** 75 min. steady ride, Z1–Z3, 45–90% FTP **Run set:** 75 min. run on rolling terrain, Z1–Z4, <104% Run FTP Last 15 min. of run are cooldown *Be in Z3, 76–90% FTP, for at least 30 min. ahead of transition. Practice fueling.*	**SWIM** **Aerobic Endurance Drills** // **2000** **Warm-up:** 800 choice **Main set:** 8 × 50 drills for technique limiter, 20 sec. rest 6 × 50 fast with good form, 30 sec. rest **Cooldown:** 500 easy

THIS IS A BIG AND IMPORTANT WEEK!

TOTAL » 14 HR. 55 MIN.

	SESSION 1	SESSION 2
Mon.	**REST DAY**	

Tues.

RUN

Neuromuscular // 50 min.

Warm-up: 35 min. Z1–Z3, 65–95% Run FTP
Main set:
6 × 200m strides, <105% Run FTP, with 200m jog recoveries
Cooldown: 5 min.
Build from slow to fast with each stride set.

SWIM

Aerobic Endurance // 3000

Warm-up: 500 easy mix of swim and kick
Main set:
3 sets:
   400 at threshold + 5 sec., 20 sec. rest
   200 pull, aerobic, 20 sec. rest
   200 steady kick, 30 sec. rest
Cooldown: 100 easy

Wed.

BIKE

Endurance Base Building // 1 hr. 10 min.

70 min. Z1/Z2, 45–75% FTP
Keep cadence high.

Thurs.

SWIM

Muscular Endurance // 3200

Warm-up: 200 swim, 100 kick, 200 pull, all with 30 sec. rest
4 × 50 drill, 15 sec. rest
Main set:
100 IM, 200 swim, each with 15 sec. rest
400 pull, 600 swim, 400 pull, all with 20 sec. rest
200 swim, 15 sec. rest
100 IM, 1 min. rest
6 × 50 fast, 30 sec. rest
Cooldown: 200 easy

STRENGTH

Pure Strength 1 // 45 min.

See p. 252 for exercises.

LEVEL 3

	SESSION 1	SESSION 2
Fri.	**BIKE** **Aerobic Recovery // 40 min.** 40 min. easy spin Z1, <56% FTP *Focus on smooth, even pedal stroke.*	**RUN** **Aerobic Recovery // 20 min.** 20 min. Z1, <75% Run FTP *Controlled and relaxed.*
Sat.	**RUN** **Aerobic Long Run // 1 hr. 10 min.** 70 min. *Get at least half of the time in Z2, 76–88% Run FTP.* *Focus on good form and quick cadence.*	**SWIM** **Aerobic Endurance Form Work // 2000** **Warm-up:** 400 choice, mix of swim and kick **Main set:** Easy effort: 6 × 100, 30 sec. rest 4 × 200 easy, 30 sec. rest **Cooldown:** 200 as 50 backstroke/50 free *Focus on form. Aim for 55–70 strokes/min.*
Sun.	**BIKE** **Endurance Recovery // 1 hr. 30 min.** 90 min. Z1/Z2, <75% FTP *Don't exceed Z2 for more than a few seconds* *at a time as when accelerating from a stop* *or going up a short hill. Comfortably high rpm.*	

LIGHTER THIS WEEK. LET THE BIG TRAINING SINK INTO THE BODY.

TOTAL » 9 HR. 5 MIN.

LEVEL 3

	SESSION 1	SESSION 2
Mon.	**STRENGTH** **Pure Strength 1 // 45 min.** *See p. 252 for exercises.*	

Tues.	**RUN**
	
	Speed Endurance // 1 hr.
	
	Warm-up: 15 min. including strides and drills
	Main set:
	4 sets:
	   1000m high Z4/low Z5a, 100–110% Run FTP,
	   2 min. rest
	   300m fast, 4 min. rest
	Cooldown: 10 min.
	Don't worry about zones on the 300s,
	just push the speed.
		SWIM
		
		Muscular Endurance // 3600
		
		Warm-up: 200 swim, 100 kick, 200 pull,
		all with 30 sec. rest
		4 × 50 drill, 15 sec. rest
		Main set:
		Rest 1 min. between sets:
		3 × 300 at threshold + 15 sec., 15 sec. rest
		3 × 300 at threshold, 15 sec. rest
		3 × 300 at threshold — 10 sec., 15 sec. rest
		Cooldown: 200 choice

Wed.	**BRICK**
	
	Bike VO$_2$max + Tempo Run //
	1 hr. 40 min.
	
	Warm-up: 20 min. ride
	Main set:
	3 sets:
	   3 × 2 min. on/90 sec. off
	   5 min. spin
	Cooldown: 15 min. spin
	Run off the bike: 20 min.
	On the bike, 2-min. "on" intervals Z5a, 121–150%
	FTP, then recover in Z1, <56% FTP; "off" intervals
	spin in Z1, <56% FTP. Set rests are also spin at Z1.
	For the run, build to Z3, 89–95% Run FTP, and
	hold steady.	

Thurs.	**SWIM** **Tri-Specific // 3000** **Warm-up:** 800 choice, a mix of swim, kick, and drills **Main set:** 4 × 400 as 200 all-out/200 steady, 3 min. rest 400 pull easy **Cooldown:** 200 very easy	**STRENGTH** **Pure Strength 1 // 45 min.** *See p. 252 for exercises.*

SESSION 1	SESSION 2
Fri.	

Fri.

RUN

Neuromuscular // 30 min.

Warm-up: 20 min. Z1/Z2, 65–88% Run FTP
Main set:
6 × 30 strides, >105% Run FTP, with walking recoveries
Cooldown: 5 min.

Strides are best done on grass or soft surface. Aim for 19–20 sec. Fast but controlled.

BIKE

Endurance Isolated-Leg Training // 1 hr.

Warm-up: 20 min.
Main set:
20 min. as 1 min. left/1 min. right
Get a total of 10 min. on each leg
Cooldown: 20 min. spin

Do this on a trainer to have non-pedaling leg on a chair. Keep comfortably high cadence. Focus on eliminating dead spot in stroke by pushing toes forward in shoes at top.

Sat.

RUN

Aerobic Rolling Course // 1 hr. 10 min.

70 min. Z1–Z3, 65–95% Run FTP

Focus on proud, upright form. Allow heart rate to gradually rise to Z3, but don't force it up.

SWIM

Aerobic Endurance // 3200

Warm-up: 200 swim, 200 stroke (no free), 200 kick, all with 30 sec. rest
Main set:
6 × 200 as 150 swim at threshold + 5 sec. per 100/50 kick, 10 sec. rest
2 min. rest
6 × 200 pull at threshold + 5 sec. per 100, 15 sec. rest
Cooldown: 200 easy

Sun.

BRICK

Bike Pyramid + Tempo Run // 2 hr. 35 min.

Warm-up: 30 min. ride
Main set:
One-to-one recovery intervals after each effort:
1 min. Z5a, 106–120% FTP, 3 min. Z4, 91–105% FTP, 6 min. high Z3, 80–90% FTP, 12 min. Z3, 76–90% FTP, 6 min. high Z3, 80–90% FTP, 3 min. Z4, 91–105% FTP, 1 min. Z5a, 106–120% FTP
Cooldown: 15 min. spin
Run off the bike: 45 min. steady

For the run, build to Z3, 89–95% Run FTP, and hold steady.

SWIM

Aerobic Endurance Drills // 2000

Warm-up: 800 choice, a mix of swim, pull, and kick
Main set:
8 × 50 drills for technique limiter, 20 sec. rest
6 × 50 fast with good form, 30 sec. rest
Cooldown: 500 easy

**THIS IS THE HIGHEST INTENSITY PHASE OF THIS PROGRAM!
FOCUS ON HITTING THE HARD WORKOUTS HARD AND THE EASY
WORKOUTS EASY. RECOVERY SHOULD BE A PRIORITY AS WELL.**

TOTAL » 13 HR. 20 MIN.

LEVEL 3

	SESSION 1	SESSION 2
Mon.	**STRENGTH** **Pure Strength 2 // 30 min.** *See p. 252 for exercises.*	
Tues.	**RUN** **Anaerobic Speed // 55 min.** **Warm-up:** 15 min. **Main set:** 3 sets: 　3 × 300m Z5a, 105–114% Run FTP, 1 min rest 　600m Z5a–Z5b, 105–125% Run FTP Rest 4 min. between sets **Cooldown:** 10 min. *Make 300s fast but controlled and 600s close to the same pace. Fast and tough!*	**SWIM** **Muscular Endurance // 2900** **Warm-up:** 200 swim, 100 kick, 200 pull, all with 30 sec. rest 4 × 50 drill or stroke, 15 sec. rest **Main set:** 5 × 100 free at threshold pace, 10 sec. rest 500 steady pull, 20 sec. rest 500 free at threshold pace, 20 sec. rest 5 × 100 free at threshold — 5 sec., 10 sec. rest **Cooldown:** 200 easy
Wed.	**BRICK** **Bike Anaerobic Capacity + Tempo Run // 1 hr. 35 min.** **Warm-up:** 20 min. ride Z1, <56% FTP **Main set:** 5 × 4 min. as 20 sec. on/10 sec. off Spin 5 min. between sets **Cooldown:** 10 min. spin **Run off the bike:** 20 min. *It's important to push very hard, 121–150+% FTP, for the 20 sec. "on" and continue to spin lightly for the 10 sec. "off." For the run, build to Z3, 89–95% Run FTP, and hold steady.*	
Thurs.	**SWIM** **Tri-Specific // 3000** **Warm-up:** 600 choice, a mix of swim and kick, 1 min. rest 6 × 50 drill, 15 sec. rest **Main set:** 2 sets: 　4 × 50 fast, 30 sec. rest 　500 steady, 15 sec. rest 　100 kick, 1 min. rest 300 pull, 20 sec. rest **Cooldown:** 200 swim	**STRENGTH** **Pure Strength 2 // 30 min.** *See p. 252 for exercises.*

	SESSION 1	SESSION 2
Fri.	**RUN**	**BIKE**
	Neuromuscular // 30 min.	**Neuromuscular Power // 1 hr.**
	Warm-up: 20 min. Z1/Z2, 65–88% Run FTP	**Warm-up:** 30 min. Z1/Z2, 45–75% FTP
	Main set:	**Main set:**
	6 × 30 strides, >105% Run FTP, with walking recoveries	8 spin-ups, 2 min. recovery
	Cooldown: 5 min.	**Cooldown:** 10 min. spin
	Strides are best done on grass or soft surface. Aim for 19–20 sec. Fast but controlled.	*When you start to bounce in the saddle, back off and recover. Don't push a big gear. Keep your legs sharp and increase cadence, not power.*
Sat.	**BRICK**	**SWIM**
	Bike Intervals + 1200m Run // 2 hr. 30 min.	**Aerobic Endurance Drills // 2000**
	Warm-up: 30 min. spin	**Warm-up:** 800 choice
	15 min. run with 4 sets of strides	**Main set:**
	Main set:	8 × 50 drills for technique limiter, 20 sec. rest
	4 sets:	6 × 50 fast with good form, 30 sec. rest
	10 min. ride Z4, 91–105% FTP, with 15 sec. spike into Z5a, >106% FTP, every 2 min.	**Cooldown:** 500 easy
	1200m run as 200m faster than race pace, building to Z5a, 105–114% Run FTP/ 800m cruising in Z4, 96–104% Run FTP/ 200m quick finish	
	Spin 5 min. between sets	
	Cooldown: 10 min. easy run	
	This workout replicates draft-legal racing with high-intensity bike-to-run efforts. Set up turbo trainer on track for quick transition.	
Sun.	**RUN**	**SWIM**
	Aerobic Base Building // 1 hr. 5 min.	**Muscular Endurance // 3300**
	65 min. Z1/Z2, 65–88% Run FTP	**Warm-up:** 400 choice, 1 min. rest;
	Light and easy with good form. Cadence at 90+ spm.	4 × 50 descend, 15 sec. rest
		Main set:
		2 sets:
		300 swim, 10 sec. rest
		3 × 100 at 100 threshold — 5 sec., 10 sec. rest
		300 pull, 20 sec. rest
		2 × 150 as 100 swim/50 kick, 30 sec. rest
		4 × 25 fast, 30 sec. rest
		Cooldown: 200 easy

TOTAL » 12 HR. 20 MIN.

WEEK 14 ◢ BUILD 2

LEVEL 3

	SESSION 1	SESSION 2
Mon.	**REST DAY**	

Tues.	**RUN**
	Test Set // 50 min.
	LTHR or RTP. See pp. 235–238 for details.
		SWIM
		Aerobic Endurance // 3250
		Warm-up: 200 swim, 100 kick, 200 pull, all with 30 sec. rest
		4 × 50 drills, 15 sec. rest
		Main set:
		8 × 250, 15 sec. rest
		   200 swim at threshold — 5 sec.
		   50 steady kick
		4 × 25 fast, 20 sec. rest
		Cooldown: 200 choice

Wed.	**BIKE** **FTP Test // 1 hr.** *If you do not have a power meter, do LTHR. See pp. 234–235 for details.*	
Thurs.	**SWIM** **STP Test // 2100** *See p. 234 for details.*	**STRENGTH** **Pure Strength 2 // 30 min.** *This is the last strength training session of the program. See p. 252 for exercises.*

	SESSION 1	SESSION 2
Fri.	**BIKE**	**RUN**
	Aerobic Recovery // 35 min.	**Aerobic Recovery // 20 min.**
	35 min. Z1, <56% FTP	20 min. Z1, <75% Run FTP
	Focus on smooth, even pedal stroke.	*Controlled and relaxed.*
Sat.	**RUN**	**SWIM**
	Aerobic Rolling Course // 1 hr.	**Aerobic Endurance Form Work // 2000**
	60 min. Z1–Z3, 65–95% Run FTP	**Warm-up:** 400 choice, a mix of swim, pull, and kick
	Focus on proud, upright form. Allow heart rate to gradually rise to Z3, but don't force it up.	**Main set:** 6 × 100 easy, 30 sec. rest 4 × 200 easy, 30 sec. rest **Cooldown:** 200 easy *Focus on form. Aim for 55–70 strokes/min.*
Sun.	**BIKE**	
	Endurance Recovery // 1 hr. 30 min.	
	90 min. Z1/Z2, 45–75% FTP	
	Don't exceed Z2 for more than a few seconds at a time as when accelerating from a stop or going up a short hill. Comfortably high rpm.	

FINAL REST AND TEST WEEK. GETTING SOME LAST FITNESS NUMBERS NAILED DOWN AND PREPARING THE BODY FOR THE FINAL PEAK PHASE OF TRAINING.

TOTAL » 8 HR. 10 MIN.

	SESSION 1	SESSION 2
Mon.	**REST DAY**	

Tues.	**RUN**
	Anaerobic Speed // 45 min.
	Warm-up: 15 min. with 8 strides
	Main set:
	8 sets:
	   300m, 45 sec. rest
	   200m build to Z5a/Z5b, 105–124% Run FTP,
	   2 min. rest
	Cooldown: 5 min.
	Focus on controlled speed. Get into Z5a, especially by the end of the 200 in each set. Follow recovery times closely—this is very important! Smooth but fast!
		SWIM
		Speed // 2500
		Warm-up: 200 swim, 100 kick, 200 pull, all with 30 sec. rest
		4 × 50 drill, 15 sec. rest; 4 × 50 descend, 15 sec. rest
		Main set:
		100 very easy swim between sets:
		2 × 200 fast, 90 sec. rest
		4 × 100 fast, 90 sec. rest
		4 × 50 fast, 1 min. rest
		4 × 25 fast, 1 min. rest
		Cooldown: 200 easy

Wed.	**BRICK** **Anaerobic Capacity + Tempo Run // 1 hr. 25 min.** **Warm-up:** 20 min. ride **Main set:** 6 × 3 min. on/3 min. off **Cooldown:** 10 min. spin **Run off the bike:** 20 min. *3 min. bike intervals should be just faster than race pace Z4/Z5a, 91–120% FTP, spinning in Z1 when "off." For the run, build to Z3, 89–95% Run FTP, and hold steady.*	
Thurs.	**SWIM** **Tri-Specific // 3000** **Warm-up:** 300 choice, 30 sec. rest; 12 × 50 as 4 × stroke/drill/fast, 15 sec. rest **Main set:** 8 × 25 fast, 30 sec. rest 4 × 200 race pace, 20 sec. rest 100 easy, 30 sec. rest 4 × 75 fast, 30 sec. rest 500 as 100 build/400 race pace 4 × 25 very fast, 30 sec. rest **Cooldown:** 100 swim	

LEVEL 3

	SESSION 1	SESSION 2
Fri.	**RUN** **Neuromuscular // 30 min.** **Warm-up:** 20 min. Z1/Z2, 65–88% Run FTP **Main set:** 6 × 30 strides, >105% Run FTP, with walking recoveries **Cooldown:** 5 min. *Strides are best done on grass or soft surface. Aim for 19–20 sec. Fast but controlled.*	**BIKE** **Aerobic Recovery // 40 min.** 40 min. Z1, <56% FTP *Focus on smooth, even pedal stroke.*

Sat.	**RUN**
	Aerobic Base Building // 50 min.
	50 min. Z1/Z2, 65–88% Run FTP
	Light and easy with good form. Cadence at 90+ spm.
		SWIM
		Speed // 1600
		Warm-up: 500 choice, 30 sec. rest; 4 × 50 drill, 15 sec. rest; 4 × 50 descend, 15 sec. rest
		Main set:
		4 sets:
		    25 as 12.5 easy/12.5 fast, 30 sec. rest
		    25 as 12.5 fast/12.5 easy, 30 sec. rest
		    25 fast, 30 sec. rest; 25 easy, 30 sec. rest
		    25 very fast, 30 sec. rest
		Rest 2 min. between sets
		Cooldown: 200 easy

Sun.	**BRICK**
	Bike Intervals + 1600m Run // 1 hr. 45 min.
	Warm-up: 30 min. ride
	Main set:
	3 sets:
	    5 min. of 15 sec. on/15 sec. off spin
	    800m run, 5 min. jog
	    800m run, 5 min. spin
	Cooldown: 10 min. jog
	Bike "on" intervals are Z5a, >106% FTP. Run immediately after, faster than race pace in high Z4/low Z5a, 100–110% Run FTP. Back off the pace to Z3, <95% Run FTP, for 5 min., then hit it again for the next 800m.
		SWIM
		Aerobic Endurance Drills // 1500
		Warm-up: 500 choice
		Main set:
		8 × 50 drills for technique limiter, 20 sec. rest
		6 × 50 fast with good form, 30 sec. rest
		Cooldown: 300 easy

NO MORE STRENGTH TRAINING. TIME TO GET SHARP AND READY TO RACE!

TOTAL » 8 HR. 50 MIN.

LEVEL 3

	SESSION 1	SESSION 2
Mon.	**REST DAY**	

Tues.

RUN

Neuromuscular // 45 min.

Warm-up: 20 min.
Main set:
6 × 1 min. accelerations, 2 min. recovery
Cooldown: 10 min.

Z1 and Z2, <88% Run FTP, for most of run.
1 min. efforts are at race pace.

SWIM

Speed // 1900

Warm-up: 300 choice, 30 sec. rest
4 × 50 drill, 15 sec. rest; 4 × 50 descend, 15 sec. rest
Main set:
100 easy swim between sets
8 × 25 as odds fast/evens easy, 30 sec. rest
4 × 50 as 25 all-out/25 easy, 30 sec. rest
4 × 50 very fast, 1 min. rest
4 × 25 very fast, 1 min. rest
Cooldown: 200 very easy

Wed.

BRICK

Bike Neuromuscular Power + Aerobic Run // 1 hr. 15 min.

Warm-up: 25 min. ride
Main set:
6 × 90 sec. accelerations on the bike, 3 min. recovery
Spin 8 min. between sets
Run off the bike: 15 min.

Build to Z5a, >106% FTP, in the bike accelerations.
For the run, just find your legs and hold steady.

Thurs.

SWIM

Speed // 2000

Warm-up: 400 choice
Main set:
4 sets:
   4 × 75 as 25 fast/25 slow/25 fast, 10 sec. rest
Rest 1 min. between sets
8 × 25 fast, 30 sec. rest
Cooldown: 200 easy

	SESSION 1	SESSION 2
Fri.	**BRICK** **Bike Neuromuscular Power +** **Aerobic Run** // 1 hr. **Main set:** 45 min. ride with 5 sec. jump once every 5 min. **Run off the bike:** 15 min. *Ride is mostly easy in Z1 and Z2, <75% FTP. Eight jumps in total, going over Z5a, >106% FTP, each time. For the run, just find your legs and hold steady.*	
Sat.	**SWIM** **Aerobic Endurance** // 700 *Check out the race swim venue if possible. Do 10 very short accelerations (25–50m) at race pace. Easy swimming between each for 30 sec. Be sure to check out the start and finish area. This is best done in the morning near race time.*	**BRICK** **Bike Accelerations +** **Run Accelerations** // 45 min. 30 min. ride 15 min. run *Do this on the race course, if possible. Include 3–4 short, race efforts. Note landmarks. Afterward, tighten all bolts on your bike.*
Sun.	**RACE DAY!**	*You've put in some great work and have prepared properly. Now, get out, execute your race plan, and have fun!*

TOTAL » **5 HR. 20 MIN. + RACE**

APPENDIX A

Test Sets

Here we have collected the test sets and calculations you will need to define the training zones used in the plans. The more accurately you can perform these sets, the better, as the information you uncover here will help guide your efforts throughout the entire plan. It is not necessary to perform all of these tests, only the tests for your level and equipment capabilities. For best results, repeat these tests every eight weeks to reestablish baselines as you improve.

SWIM THRESHOLD PACE (STP) TEST

500 easy swim warm-up

5 × 100 descend each, 20 sec. rest

1000 time trial

Be sure to pace yourself, but consider this race effort, leaving nothing left.

At the end of the time trial, find the average pace per 100 meters/yards.

200 easy cooldown

Calculate Your Swim Zones from STP Test

The average 100 meter/yard pace from the 1000 meter/yard test is your swim threshold pace (STP).

ZONE 1 ▶ Aerobic/Recovery (> STP +30 sec.)

ZONE 2 ▶ Endurance (STP +15–29 sec.)

ZONE 3 ▶ Intensive Endurance (STP +7–14 sec.)

ZONE 4 ▶ Sub-Threshold (STP +1–6 sec.)

ZONE 5

  A ▶ Threshold (STP to STP -3 sec.)

  B ▶ Anaerobic Endurance (STP -4–10 sec.)

  C ▶ Power (< STP -11 sec.)

BIKE FUNCTIONAL THRESHOLD POWER (FTP) TEST

30 min. easy warm-up

5 min. *max* effort

5 min. easy spin above 90 pedal revolutions per minute (rpm)

20 min. *max* effort

Be sure to pace yourself so you finish strong, but consider this race effort on flat, uninterrupted terrain.

Hit "stop" at the end of the second *max* effort and record the average power of the 20 min. effort in watts.

Calculate Your Bike Zones from FTP Test

Your functional threshold power (FTP) is determined by multiplying the average power from the previous 20-minute test by 0.95. If your average power was 300 watts, you would calculate FTP as $300 \times 0.95 = 285$ watts. Use that value to determine your power zones for cycling.

ZONE 1 ▶ Active Recovery (< 56% of FTP)

ZONE 2 ▶ Endurance (56–75% of FTP)

ZONE 3 ▶ Tempo (76–90% of FTP)

ZONE 4 ▶ Lactate Threshold (91–105% of FTP)

ZONE 5 ▶ VO$_2$max (106–120% of FTP)

ZONE 6 ▶ Anaerobic Capacity (121–150% of FTP)

ZONE 7 ▶ Neuromuscular Power (> 150% of FTP)

BIKE OR RUN LACTATE THRESHOLD HEART RATE (LTHR) TEST

If you don't have a heart-rate monitor, use this as a benchmark test, trying to improve on your total distance over the time trial from one test to the next.

20 min. warm-up

30 min. time trial

Be sure to pace yourself, but consider this race effort.

After the 10 min. mark, press the lap button on your watch
and capture the heart rate for the final 20 min.

Calculate Your Bike Zones from LTHR Test

The average heart rate from the final 20 minutes of the test will be approximately at or just below your lactate threshold. Use that value to determine your zones for cycling.

ZONE 1 ▶ Aerobic/Recovery (< 81% of LTHR)

ZONE 2 ▶ Endurance (81–89% of LTHR)

ZONE 3 ▶ Intensive Endurance (90–93% of LTHR)

ZONE 4 ▶ Sub-Threshold (94–99% of LTHR)

ZONE 5

A ▶ Threshold (100–102% of LTHR)

B ▶ Anaerobic Endurance (103–106% of LTHR)

C ▶ Power (> 106% of LTHR)

Calculate Your Run Zones from LTHR Test

The average heart rate from the final 20 minutes of the test will be approximately at or just below your lactate threshold. Use that value to determine your zones for running.

ZONE 1 ▸ Aerobic/Recovery (< 85% of LTHR)

ZONE 2 ▸ Endurance (85–89% of LTHR)

ZONE 3 ▸ Intensive Endurance (90–94% of LTHR)

ZONE 4 ▸ Sub-Threshold (95–99% of LTHR)

ZONE 5

    A ▸ Threshold (100–102% of LTHR)

    B ▸ Anaerobic Endurance (103–106% of LTHR)

    C ▸ Power (> 106% of LTHR)

RUN MAX HEART RATE (MHR) TEST

While this test can be performed on any flat, uninterrupted, and measured course, for best results, perform it on a track with each effort performed immediately after the one before it—no rest or break between.

20 min. warm-up with 4 sets of strides (p. 249), building in intensity

1 mile hard effort, gradually building from an easy RPE of 10,
    but finishing the mile at a hard (but not all-out) tempo

400m, increasing the pace every 100 meters,
    finishing the final 100 at maximum, all-out effort

10 min. cooldown, very easy

Record the highest heart rate from the session (most heart rate monitors
    have a "max heart rate" function for each workout)

Calculate Your Run Zones from the MHR Test

Using the max heart rate from the test, plug the values into this chart to determine your zones for running.

ZONE 1 ▶ Aerobic/Recovery (< 74% of Max Heart Rate)

ZONE 2 ▶ Endurance (74–79% of MHR)

ZONE 3 ▶ Intensive Endurance (80–83% of MHR)

ZONE 4 ▶ Sub-Threshold (84–89% of MHR)

ZONE 5

    A ▶ Threshold (90–93% of MHR)

    B ▶ Anaerobic Endurance (94–97% of MHR)

    C ▶ Power (98–100% of MHR)

RUN THRESHOLD PACE (RTP) TEST

20 min. easy warm-up, then hit "start" on your watch and go right into 3 mile/5K time trial

Be sure to pace yourself, but consider this race effort on flat, uninterrupted terrain.

Hit "stop" at the end of the *max* effort and record the time and average pace (in minutes per mile).

Strap on your math caps—the easiest way to calculate the run zone paces from RTP uses this formula:

Convert RTP into seconds
 (RTP of mm:ss becomes mm × 60 + ss), then
RTP seconds × zone percentage = RTP zone
RTP zone—RTP (in seconds) = RTP difference
RTP difference + RTP (in mm:ss) = zone pace

For example, to find lower-end zone 3 pace from an RTP of 7:15/mile:

7 minutes × 60 + 15 seconds = 435 seconds
435 × 0.88 (lower percentage of zone 3 is 88%) = 382.8
382.8—435 = -52.2
-52.2 + 7:15 = lower-end pace of zone 3 is 6:22.8

Calculate Your Run Zones from RTP Test

The average mile pace from the previous 3-mile or 5K test is your Run Threshold Pace (RTP).

ZONE 1 ▶ Aerobic/Recovery (< 79% of RTP)

ZONE 2 ▶ Endurance (79–87% of RTP)

ZONE 3 ▶ Intensive Endurance (88–94% of RTP)

ZONE 4 ▶ Sub-Threshold (95–100% of RTP)

ZONE 5

    A ▶ Threshold (101–103% of RTP)

    B ▶ Anaerobic Endurance (104–109% of RTP)

    C ▶ Power (110% of RTP)

RUN FUNCTIONAL THRESHOLD POWER (RFTP) TEST

20-minute warm-up with 6 sets of strides (p. 249)

2 × 10 minutes at *max* effort. Be sure to pace yourself so you finish strong,
    but consider this race effort on flat, uninterrupted terrain.

Between each effort, take 2 minutes to stand, stretch, and walk.

For each *max* effort, record the distance, average heart rate,
    and average power.

Calculate Your Run Zones from RFTP Test

Your run functional threshold power (Run FTP) is determined by multiplying the average power from the two previous 10-minute tests by 0.95. If your average power for the first test was 200 watts and the average power for the second test was 210 watts, you would calculate your Run FTP as roughly (200 + 210) / 2 × 0.95 = 195 watts. Use that value to determine your power zones for running.

ZONE 1 ▸ Active Recovery (<75% of FTP)

ZONE 2 ▸ Endurance (76–88% of FTP)

ZONE 3 ▸ Tempo (89–95% of FTP)

ZONE 4 ▸ Lactate Threshold (96–104% of FTP)

ZONE 5 ▸ VO$_2$max (105–114% of FTP)

ZONE 6 ▸ Anaerobic Capacity (115–124% of FTP)

ZONE 7 ▸ Neuromuscular Power (>125% of FTP)

APPENDIX B

Swimming Drills

These drills should be performed at various times before your swim training—based on identifying key weaknesses from pp. 44–49. Ideally, work on a few drills during each session's warm-up phase in order to best focus on your particular swimming issue. Immediately following each drill, be intentional about focusing on that drilled area as you swim your workout set.

STREAMLINING

Dedicate time to practice pushing off the wall (flip turn or no), making your body as long and taut as possible. The goal is to hold this streamline position as long—and as far—as you can to maintain optimal body position while swimming.

SIDE-TO-SIDE DRILL (7-BEAT KICK)

While looking down at the bottom of the pool, swim on your side with one arm extended out and one by your side. Kick seven times on one side, pull, rotate to the other side, then repeat. This drill helps with rotation and catch.

ONE-ARM DRILL (BOTH ARMS OUT)

Same as above, but breathe to the side that is pulling through. Focus on grabbing the water and keeping a high elbow in one strong, fluid motion. The emphasis is on catching the water with the pulling arm. Do 25 pulling with one arm, 25 with the other.

HIGH ELBOW

Keep your elbow as high underwater as you can while otherwise swimming normally. Visualize it just barely skimming the air above.

FINGERTIP DRAG

While swimming normally, let your fingertips drag across the surface of the water as you bring your hand forward with each stroke, and focus on a high elbow.

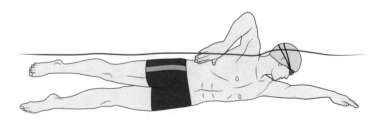

ZIPPER DRILL

Another high-elbow recovery drill, run your thumb along the side of your body as you bring your arm forward on each stroke. When your thumb gets to your ear, finish the stroke and begin the same motion with the other arm.

FIST DRILL

Swim normally, holding a clenched fist. You'll need to focus on using the flat part of your forearm to move you through the water instead of your hand—this works both the catch and pull phases.

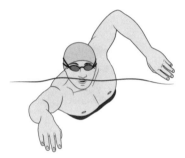

TARZAN DRILL

Swimming with your head up out of the water is crucial in open-water swimming. Practice this, keeping your eyes just above the water to see and raising your mouth every few strokes to breathe. As you sight, notice where your hands enter the water and if your elbows are high during the catch phase.

HESITATION DRILL

Swim normally, pausing for a little less than a second halfway through your recovery phase, while your hand is midway out of the water. During the pause, focus on keeping your hips high in the water by adjusting your body position and keeping your midsection taut.

APPENDIX C

Running Drills

These drills, specified before each running workout, will loosen up the muscles, get blood pumping to the heart, and—most importantly—prime your body for proper running form and technique. Do not rush these movements, but rather be intentional about each one. Aside from making each run faster and more efficient, these drills will also help with injury prevention by reminding your fatigued body of proper technique. Note: Some drills specify reps.

ANKLING

Strike the ground immediately beneath you with your forefoot, and lower your heel to the ground, barely making contact. Using a quick, short, low stride, bring your foot up off the ground, as if the ground is hot and you are barefoot. This drill helps promote proper leg loading while running. Be sure to keep your arms tight and compact to help match the speed of your foot-strike with the speed of your arm swing.

ANKLE SPRINGS

Run very short, quick steps with feet flat on the ground and stiff ankles. Unlike the ankling drill, this does not put you on your toes. Be sure to quickly swing your foot beneath you and imagine "popping" your lower leg forward.

RUSSIAN DRILL

Similar to ankle springs, run with a straight leg, visualizing marching like a soldier with a moderate-length stride. Unlike ankle springs, lightly scrape your forefoot on the ground as you bring each foot back beneath you.

HIGH KNEES

Focusing more on the pulling up than the landing (again imagining the ground is hot), keep on your toes and pull your knees up toward your chest with a moderate-length stride. Lean forward with eyes gazing straight ahead, and resist the urge to let your shoulders fall backward. Keep swinging your arms as if you were running normally.

BUTT KICKS

Bring your heels up underneath you—not behind you—with quick, short steps. Focus on relaxing your quads and engaging your hamstrings as much as possible with very quick feet.

SKIPPING WITH HIGH KNEES

Using the same form as in high knees, do a small skip where you take off and land on the same foot for a moment before switching legs at a short stride. Think about popping off the ground quickly and making the change in rhythm.

LEG EXTENSIONS

These should look similar to skipping with high knees, but with the raised leg kicking out in front, becoming nearly straight. This can take work to time properly, but it helps to think of it as a skip to get the knee high, followed by another movement to kick out, then finally scraping the extended foot on the ground before returning.

TOE TAPS

Tap your left foot down with a fast, light movement while hopping with a very short stride. The moment it touches the ground, lift the left knee, as if doing high knees; bring back down for another tap. Do 15 repeats, then switch legs.

TOE-HAND TAPS

Do the same as in toe taps, but when you bring your foot up with a high knee, touch the inside arch of your foot with the opposite hand. Do 15 on one side, 15 on the other.

QUICK FEET

Using a long, straight line (on a track works quite well), take one quick step to the right, immediately following with the left foot, almost touching the right. Step back with the left foot, then with the right. Repeat on the other side, always returning to center as fast—and as lightly—as possible. Do 30 total.

STRIDES

Do an 80- to 100-yard run at mile pace with perfect form, focusing more on running *well* than running *fast*; full recovery between each set.

APPENDIX D

Strength Workouts

Every strength session follows the same workout structure involving the movements detailed in Chapter 4 (pp. 69–75). Only the number of sets, repetitions, weight, and recovery varies. Before all strength workouts, be sure to warm up for 10 minutes with easy running or spinning. The strength exercises are done as supersets, so you will do all of the sets (between 1 and 3) of a single superset before moving on to the next superset. For example, if you were in the Anatomical Adaptation phase of strength training (described on the following page), you would do a set of 20 lunges and 20 shoulder shrugs, rest 45 seconds, and repeat the set two more times, again resting between sets. Then you would move on to the leg press and bicep curls superset.

ANATOMICAL ADAPTATION

Choose a lighter weight. The goal is not to lift to failure or fatigue—you could likely double the reps before reaching failure.

> 3 sets of 20 reps of each strength superset; rest 45 seconds between sets

FITNESS STRENGTH

Choose a moderate weight. The last set of each exercise should be feeling relatively hard.

> 3 sets of 15 reps of each strength superset; rest 45 seconds between sets

PURE STRENGTH 1

Choose a moderate to heavy weight. Add weight to the second set if needed.

> **SET 1** ▷ 10 reps of each strength superset; rest 90 seconds between sets
> **SET 2** ▷ 6 reps of each strength superset to fatigue (not failure)
> **CORE PROGRAM** ▷ 3 sets of 30 reps (1 round of each core exercise is 1 set)

PURE STRENGTH 2

Choose a heavy weight. The goal is to lift to fatigue, but with perfect form.

> 1 set of 8 reps of each strength superset; rest 90 seconds between sets
> **CORE PROGRAM** ▷ 3 sets of 30 reps (1 round of each core exercise is 1 set)

STRENGTH PROGRAM

1

LUNGES (p. 69)

SHOULDER SHRUGS (p. 69)

2

LEG PRESS (p. 70)

BICEP CURL (p. 70)

3

DEAD LIFT (p. 71)

ROMAN CHAIR (always 30 reps, p. 71)

4

SEATED HAMSTRING CURL
(p. 72)

LAT PULL-DOWN (p. 72)

5

LEG ABDUCTION/ADDUCTION
(p. 73)

CORE PROGRAM

CRUNCHES (p. 74) A full set of up, left, right counts as 3 reps.

ELEVATED-LEG CRUNCHES (p. 74) A full set of up, left, right counts as 3 reps.

SIDE OBLIQUE CRUNCHES (p. 75)

HIP ROLL (p. 75)

LEG-EXTENSION CORE (p. 75)

Acknowledgments

As someone who clearly gravitates toward relatively short things, writing a book is pretty far outside of my comfort zone. But just like anything that forces you to step up in length—the mile in elementary school, 10K in college, two-hour races in tri—you end up learning a ton about yourself. Yes, this project has felt more like a quadruple, multistage ultra-decathlon when compared to the usual magazine writing I do at *Triathlete*, but I'm glad to have given it a shot. Maybe I'm a short-course athlete and a long-course writer!

First off, I'd like to thank my wife, Karli, whose patience with my boundless multisport ADD has allowed me to pursue a career in sports for much longer than I (or anyone?) would have thought. With this book in particular, her understanding allowed me to disappear into the desert for days on end to write and run and write and run and still come back feeling loved.

I'd also like to give a humongous thanks to Ryan Bolton, someone I barely knew before we began this process together, but whose legend preceded him. It's rare to be able to work with someone who's an incredible athlete, an incredible coach, and an incredibly patient (and thorough) collaborator. This book is as much his as it is mine. I'd also like to thank one of my best friends, Casey Maguire, not only for his work on this book, but for his endless support during what could have been a train wreck of a year.

I'd like to thank the team at Pocket Outdoor Media: First, Erin Beresini, for not only taking a chance on hiring a former pro/freelancer as a senior editor, but also for setting the book bar high by writing one of her own. I'd like to thank Renee Jardine for her encouragement and guidance—despite her insanely full plate. I'd also like to thank the editorial and production team—Casey Blaine, Andrea Dehnke, Sarah Gorecki, and Vicki Hopewell—for their endless patience around my goofy schedule.

Finally, I'd like to thank the triathlon community for supporting me as I raced—and for listening to what I had to say when I stopped. Yes, the multisport tribe can sometimes feel intense and exclusive, but at the end of the day, I think we can all admit that none of us really know what we're doing.

About the Authors

Chris Foster is the senior editor at *Triathlete* magazine, and a former NCAA Division I runner and professional short-course triathlete. He has a journalism degree from Penn State University, and currently lives, works, trains, and coaches high school cross-country in Los Angeles.

Ryan Bolton coaches every level of triathlete and runner, from world-class professionals and Olympians to first-timers. He is the founder of the Harambee Project in Santa Fe, New Mexico, a group of elite distance runners. A former collegiate runner, Bolton was also a pro triathlete and was a member of the very first US Olympic team in triathlon in 2000.

Casey Maguire is a Los Angeles–based orthopedic physical therapist who has treated professional triathletes, cyclists, and athletes in the NBA, NHL, NFL, and USTA. His focus is on functional biomechanics.